To Jeff

Make happy memories
They last the rest of
your life

Nina Moore

An American Love Story

by
Mina Moore

authorHOUSE

AuthorHouse™
1663 Liberty Drive, Suite 200
Bloomington, IN 47403
www.authorhouse.com
Phone: 1-800-839-8640

© 2007 Mina Moore. All rights reserved.
No part of this book may be reproduced, stored in a retrieval system, or transmitted by any means without the written permission of the author.

First published by AuthorHouse 5/16/2007

ISBN: 978-1-4343-1311-9 (sc)

Printed in the United States of America
Bloomington, Indiana
This book is printed on acid-free paper.

Library of Congress Control Number: 2007903394

This book is dedicated to my beloved husband, Bill Moore.

Introduction

My name is Mina Moore. My husband Bill and I were inseparable for more than 50 years. This is the story of how my husband and I spent our life together. Too many people go through life trying to accumulate only wealth; we spent a lifetime acquiring memories. When I sit back and realize all that we did in our life, no money in the world could ever replace or enhance what we accomplished. I am thankful for every day.

It is amazing to sit back and think about the history of this country. Either my husband or I have lived through every major event in America in the past 80 years. We remembered the stock market crash that led to the Great Depression and I witnessed the Dot.com bubble burst 70 years later. We rode in horse drawn carriages, and we watched men land on the moon and the space shuttle take flight. I remember when I saw my first radio and black and white television, and I now receive pictures of my great grandchildren via e-mail.

When I was young, I remember it seemed like the Yankees were in the World Series every year and…oh wait, bad example.

I invite you all to come along for the ride. I hope you enjoy reading this book as much as I enjoyed reflecting on our life together.

Mina Moore

Chapter 1
Our Childhood

It is difficult to understand our life together without having background on our childhood. My husband, Bill Moore, did not have an easy life. He was born on October 1, 1923, in Farmington, Connecticut. His mother, Louise, emigrated from Holland in 1910. She arrived via boat from Europe, passed through Ellis Island with her family, and settled in Ridgewood, New Jersey. Louise was originally married to a man named John Schlegel, and they had three daughters over a 12-year span. Bill was never clear on the details of where his mother's first marriage ended and the next one began, but she later married Bill's father, William John Moore, who was a laborer on a peach farm.

When Bill was 2 years old, his father abandoned his family, leaving Louise to raise Bill and his three sisters alone. At the time, Minnie was 7, Helen was 9, and Ruth was 11. Bill was by far the youngest in the family. Their life experiences profoundly affected each child who trailed them throughout their lives. Minnie was always Bill's favorite sister and lived the most normal life of the girls. She married a bus driver in Patterson, New Jersey, in the 1930s and had four children of her own. Her husband died at the age of 65. Helen married a soldier in 1942 but divorced him when he came home from the war in poor health after contracting malaria. She was always more of a "girl about town," which Bill detested. Ruth faced the most difficulty in her life. Her adopted father sexually abused her. Unfortunately, her mother knew about the situation but did nothing to prevent it. Once she was of age, Ruth moved to Boston, discovered she was a lesbian, and lived the rest of her life with her companion. She also found time to have a child of her own.

After his father left the family, Bill never saw him again. When Bill was fourteen, his mother learned that William was killed in a car accident in upstate New York. He was buried in a pauper's grave.

One of the few recollections Bill had of any type of kinship was watching his maternal grandfather cut off the end of a cigar with a little knife. Bill was given the knife as a young child, and it was one of his most prized possessions throughout his life. He in turn passed this knife down to his grandson, Dan.

Life seemed to get more difficult by the year for the Moore family as the Great Depression enveloped the country. "Moms," as we called Louise, could not keep the family together. Ruth, the oldest daughter, was given up for adoption at the age of 12 to a childless couple acquainted with the family. It was Moms' hope that this would at least enable her to keep in touch with Ruth. Even though Ruth's adoptive father abused her, she still kept in touch with her mother, and they remained in contact throughout their lives.

Moms' other two daughters were sent to a place called Vall-Halla – a trade school of sorts. There they learned household duties so they could obtain work as maids or live-in domestic servants. They were sent to work in family homes around Ridgewood.

Bill was sent to a home for poor children on Long Island, where he lived from the time he was 4 until he was 8 years old. He never said much about the home. From what little he described, it was similar to an orphanage. The boys slept in a group area similar to a barracks and ate in a mess hall. Bill never provided me with much detail about this part of his life. He just left it to say that they were not treated very well. One of the few things he mentioned was that every Saturday they had to line up for cod liver oil, which was the 1920s answer to a multivitamin.

Bill missed his mother but she could not afford to go to Long Island to visit him. The trip would have taken about three hours at that time because the George Washington Bridge had not yet been built. In order to get from New Jersey to Long Island, she would have needed to take a ferry across the Hudson River and drive through New York City. When he could finally come home, Bill did not even recognize his own mother. He actually ran to the social worker instead of Moms.

Moms was able to bring Bill home when she took a job with The Wilsons, a wealthy family in Ridgewood. They had a mentally disabled 20-year-old son, and Moms and Bill were both allowed to live at the house as long as they took care of the child. Bill was only 8 years old, but he was told to play with the boy, whose favorite game was to sit on the floor and roll a ball back and forth. Finally the Depression caught up with this family as well, and after four years, Bill and his mother had to move out.

At the time I met Bill, he was living together with Moms, Helen, and Minnie in a small apartment in Ridgewood. Minnie married soon afterwards, which left Moms, Helen, and Bill. Moms scraped by working as a domestic servant, and their income was supplemented by welfare, which mostly amounted to food donations. Life was not too easy for Bill in this situation. Moms and Helen each had nice large bedrooms with maple bedroom suites. Bill's room was about the size of a closet with a link spring bed and a two-inch mattress. Bill's most challenging difficulty at home was the men that both his mother and Helen quite often brought home to spend the night. Bill stayed in the attic of the store next to their apartment to get away from it all. The attic lacked both heat and electricity; it had just a mattress on the floor and some rats to keep him company.

Bill went to school during the day and ran a paper route after school. Bill also made money by walking along the railroad tracks picking up loose coal that had fallen from the trains passing by town. His mother tried to make some money by selling pepper hash made out of red and greens peppers and onions. Of course Bill had to help out by grinding the peppers and onions. During the summer, Bill would search local farms to find peaches that had dropped on the ground. He would bring them home and skin them so his mother could make jam. Although he never made much money at his odd jobs, Bill just accepted the fact and gave what little he made to his mother (minus cigarette money). Even when Bill was in high school and held several different jobs and made more money, he still gave up most of his earnings to support his family. Even at a young age, he felt a responsibility as the only male in the house to be somewhat of a provider.

During summer vacations from school, Bill was sent to live on farms to pick fruits and vegetables. The kids in the neighborhood informed each other of which farmers were looking for temporary workers to bring in the harvest. His hardest job was on a farm in Franklin Lakes, New Jersey, about twelve miles from his home in Ridgewood. Bill was picking raspberries, but he actually liked eating them more than picking the berries. To end this problem, the boys were made to whistle while they picked the berries so the crew leader would know they were not eating the crop. One day when they were going to the fields from the farmhouse, the owner slammed the car door on Bill's fingers. When Bill yelled out, "My fingers are caught in the door," the farmer told him to shut up and that he should not have put his fingers in the door in the first place. The cruel bastard did not open up the door until they reached the field. Bill now had three twisted fingers. When I fell in love with Bill and heard these stories, I just wanted to hug him and never let him go. Bill worked every summer until high school on either a berry farm or a farm in Paramus harvesting celery.

Because Moms was still on welfare, a social worker used to come by announced and spot check the apartment. It was on one of these occasions that Bill, at age twelve, was caught smoking. The social worker accused him of trying to set the apartment on fire. As punishment, he had to ride his bike every Saturday morning to the jail in Hackensack, New Jersey, for a year. This trip was eight miles in each direction. He did not have to work; he just had to report to the prison matron in charge of the female inmates and juvenile delinquents. The matron of the prison took a liking to Bill. Every Saturday they ended up having long talks about life. They would have discussions on topics such as "Have pride in yourself because the inner you is what counts," or "Life doesn't owe you a thing. You have to earn it." Out of these sessions, I truly believe Bill learned to be the good husband and father he turned out to be. When I moved to Ridgewood four years later, I met the social worker. She always figured she was punishing Bill, when actually she was helping him in more ways than she ever realized. Unfortunately, I must admit that helping him was not likely her true intention.

Another part of Bill's life that made me so upset was the accusations made against him because of his background. Whenever the police had a problem in town, they always seemed to knock on Bill's door first to see where he was at the time in question. Just because he was poor and from a bad family, the police seemed to feel they had the right to do this on many different occasions. Their suspicions were never right. Most of the time, Bill's alibi was being at work, and it was easy for the police to verify it.

I asked Bill how he decided to make the choices he did about his life and why he didn't turn out to be a hoodlum or petty thief. Bill chose to rise above his upbringing to become a good man. His answer on how he accomplished this surprised me. He said, "I watched people in real life that I admired and tried to copy them." For instance, at my parents home, he watched how my father ate in such a distinguished manner and developed the same habit. He also said that he would see how loving couples acted towards each other, and that he knew he wanted someone to love him like that. He certainly did find someone to really love him the rest of his life. I do not want to make Bill out to be something he wasn't. He did have the proverbial Irish temper, and it came out on occasion over the years. Bill also hated to lose at anything. Bill, however, always reminded me that his anger was not directed at me, but at the situation. I am a firm believer that you cannot change people. You accept them for who they are. I always felt his good points far exceeded his bad points.

I always held my Bill up on a pedestal because of the way he prevented how he could have, and probably should have, turned out. By his own doing, he took responsibility for his own life and made a man of himself. I feel that at the minute we met, we had such a love for each other that, side by side, we were ready to tackle anything that fate threw at us.

My younger years were quite a bit different than Bill's. I was born in Garfield, New Jersey, on February 27, 1924, to Robert and Jessie Haessner. My mother was born in Holland and came to America as a teenager in 1912 with her parents and four sisters. My parents were married in 1917 in Philadelphia, Pennsylvania, where my father worked in a shipyard during World War I. They remained married for 48 years. They had three children during their lifetime. My parent's first son, Walter, died before I was born at the age of 6 from mastoiditis. This was a serious inflammation in the neck that developed into a terrible infection. Before antibiotics, this was a disease that was commonly fatal. Their second son, my brother Bill, is four years older than me.

My father was born in Passaic, New Jersey, but was sent to Germany for his schooling. He lived in the rural valley of Alsas Lorraine with his aunt throughout his school years. The schools in Germany were much more formal than those in the United States and concentrated on schoolwork over extracurricular activities. My father was schooled abroad because he was expected to follow in his father's footsteps and enter the textile industry. My grandfather originally worked for Mr. J Forstmann in Germany and later opened a Forstmann Woolen Company in Garfield, New Jersey. Later, my father would become the head designer for the New Jersey location and held this job for the rest of his life.

Forstmann Woolens produced some of the finest wool material in the world. Some of the textiles produced by the Forstmann Company have been used to produce garments for royal families all over the world, including the Queen of England. In 1928, at the beginning of the Great Depression, the wool sold for $15 per yard. Even during this difficult economic time, our family did not have any financial problems.

Although the wool my father's company produced contained wonderful colors and textures, they were designed for older and more mature tastes. Unfortunately, my mother decided that she was going to make all of my clothes out of this material or take the materials to a tailor to design my wardrobe. I would have much rather worn the bright plaids and checks that were popular in the day, but those types of designs were unheard of at Forstmanns.

One of my earlier memories of my father was watching him work on a design on the dining room table at night. He would fill in tiny 1/8 inch by 1/8 inch squares to make a pattern. I was 8 years old at the time, and I climbed up next to him to watch him work. I grabbed some of sheets and colored them in with a crayon and gave him a new pattern to take to work to make into a skirt for me. He was not impressed with my design work and chased me from the table.

My father was 6 feet tall with dark hair and blue eyes. He was a very distinguished looking man as well as very well mannered with a wonderful sense of humor. He always wore dark suits with white shirts – never colored – along with conservative ties and shoes that were polished daily. In his spare time he loved to garden and fish.

Everyone who met my father seemed to like him very much, including his two sisters-in-law. The people who worked for him idolized him and would bend over backwards to help him. In return, he treated the people that worked for him with a great deal of respect and cared about their problems. His secretary began her first job working for my father and ended up working for him for her entire life. When I was young, my father would take me to the mill from time to time. I really liked this because everyone made such a fuss over me. I did not realize at the time that it was because I was the daughter of the boss. He called everyone by his or her first name and his employees called him Bob, so I just assumed he was one of the guys.

Unfortunately, we had a very quarrelsome family at home. My brother could not handle all of the arguing, so he was seldom at home. He was only there to eat and sleep. Otherwise, he spent his time playing various sports at the YMCA and Boys Clubs with his friend Hans. I, on the other hand, had to listen to my mother constantly run down my father, whom I loved dearly. She made me responsible for making her happy and demanded that I be with her at all times. I had no choice but to sit around and listen to her complain about her unhappiness, and the conversation always turned to my father. She would constantly complain about everything he did for the family.

I could not have any friends over to the house, nor could I go over to their homes. She would tell me, "Mommy needs you because you are all I have." She never went with my father to any of the affairs the Forstmanns's had for the employees. Our vacations were just as miserable because she complained about everything: the hotel, the food, the other guests, the staff. Even at our summer cabin she made herself just as miserable. The only time I got away was when I snuck out behind her back. My mother never let up on my father, and it eventually affected my health as well as my father's. My mother even tried going to a psychiatrist but it did not help. I once asked my father how he could take it for all of those years, and he replied, "I love her." I learned that money does not bring happiness. Fortunately, after meeting Bill, I realized that love does.

In 1928, my father purchased a lot where we built a summer cabin near Lake Erskine, New Jersey. We would head out every year after the last day of school. We packed up the Model T with our clothes and our bird, Hansy. It was about a 25-mile ride from our home, but it seemed to take most of the day. There were no roads traveling directly to the cabin, so it was a round-a-bout drive. My father stayed in town during the week and came out on the weekends because the drive made it difficult to commute to work each day.

There were three large lakes in the area: Lake Erskine, Cupsaw Lake, and Upper Lake. Each lake was big enough to handle the motorboats owned by the residents in the area. The lakes were surrounded by several hundred homes – some permanent and some for summer or weekend use. There was very little cost to constructing our cabin, which was a block from the lake. The male members of our family as well as neighbors around the lake helped to build it. This entitled our family members to come up and enjoy themselves at the lake whenever they had a chance. In return, my Dad helped the neighbors whenever they had a project to be finished around their cabins. Our cabin had a kitchen, two bedrooms, a front room with a balcony where my brother slept, and an "L" porch that went around two sides of the house. Outside, my father would use the tree to mount the bass fish he caught in the lake.

At the end of the summer, Dad always threw a party for the family and neighbors. I do not want to guess how much beer was consumed at these parties, but it was always enough for plenty of mischief. One year, the men rolled huge boulders up against the back of Dad's car so he could not get out of the driveway.

Many German families from the Garfield, New Jersey, area had cabins on this lake. Many of these people worked for my father at the mill. Even today, the German community still flourishes around Lake Erskine and the surrounding areas. Many of the homes built around the lake today are owned by third generation families of people I knew back in the 1930s.

My brother became close friends with a boy named Hans Khroler, whose family had a cabin across from ours. The family had a main house where they cooked and congregated, which was surrounded by little one-room cabins to sleep in. These people amazed me by the way they took care of each other. Hans' father fought for Germany in World War I; he was gassed and never really recovered. The entire group took care of him. Bill H and Hans developed a close friendship that would last a lifetime. When they were in their young teens, both Hans and my brother were so skinny I thought we could almost see through them. As they got older, Hans became quite a handsome young man, and I developed my first crush on him. Unfortunately, Hans was 16 and I was 11 so to him, I was his little sister. As a matter fact, one time Hans was teasing me so much about being his little sister that I punched him as hard as I could and ended up giving him a whopper of a black eye. Hans and my brother laughed themselves silly about it for years to come. Even after Hans joined the Navy, whenever he returned on leave, the story of the black eye was sure to resurface.

At the lake, I would always try my best to hang out with my brother and his friends. It did not always work, but they would watch over me. If any of the other boys teased me, especially for my fear of diving off of the high board, they would suddenly find themselves with a black eye, courtesy of one of my many protectors. If I did get to spend the day with my brother, it was always an adventure. I believed everything he and his friends said; it was true hero worship. If the day called for swinging on hanging grapevines, they said I had to test them by going first to be sure they would hold us up. Meanwhile, I would be swinging over a ledge, hoping for the best. When we walked across a bog field, they would tell me not to slip because we were surrounded by quicksand. I was so gullible and so afraid at the same time.

We would also take long hikes into the woods surrounding the lake. One path led us to a wide and fairly deep creek. Since I was only 7, I did not think twice about taking off my clothes and swimming across with my outfit wadded up in a ball, balanced above both the water and my head. Innocence is wonderful at that age. I also learned to swim like a fish at an early age. If I was in a rowboat with my brother, invariably

I would find myself tossed out into the water, forced to swim the rest of the way back to shore. At least they would stay close enough to pull me in if I got too tired.

We used to hike to a place called Skyland Farm, which was an old abandoned estate with a stone mansion about five miles from the lake. It is amazing to think about now, but we would head out on a five-mile hike without any food or water. We would just hike, eating berries along the way and drinking from streams. Bill and Hans were very familiar with the outdoors. Being excellent woodsmen, they knew which types of plants were edible, and we never got sick from any of the water we drank.

The backyard of Skyland Farm had an old pond with murky water that contained hungry fish about five inches long. My brother told me to put my hand in the water to see if the pond contained piranhas. Obviously, kids have been mean to each other for many years. Since I was young but wanted to act tough, I put my hand in to find out. The fish nibbled on my hand, but that was all. My brother and Hans would jump into the water and rush to the ladder to pull themselves out as soon as possible, competing to see who had the most fish bites on their body. Luckily, I missed out on that adventure.

Our one and only fishing expedition took a turn for the worse when Hans cast his line and accidentally hooked me in the cheek. Fishing hooks really need to be worked to come loose. As they tried to unhook me from the line, they kept looking at me saying, "Don't you dare cry." I never cried that day, but I also never went fishing with them again.

I really have some wonderful memories of my early childhood. I remember running outside at the sound of an airplane to watch the spectacular sight. In 1928, the skies were not alive with constant motion like today. When we heard an airplane overhead, it was such an unusual sound we raced outside to look. We usually saw small planes covered in fabric with room for the pilot and one passenger. Once in a great while, we would see a larger metal plane that carried a dozen people or so. We would watch these planes with awe, thinking it was simply an unbelievable sight. I, of course, thought there was no way anyone could ever get me into such a dangerous contraption. We were so young and aviation was still in its infancy, so we were unaware of the different types of aircraft. We just referred to all of them as airplanes.

One of our hobbies was following the iceman's wagon. Before people had refrigerators, the iceman would come by every house to see if they needed a 10 cent or 15 cent piece of ice. He would chip off the piece, grab it with ice tongs, and place it in the icebox. The kids in the neighborhood would gather around the iceman, and he would give us the small chips that fell from the ice block. They tasted awful, essentially amounting to a dirty ice slushee. On other days, we would follow the fish wagon and hold our noses at him, yelling, "You stink!"

One of the best memories was beating Mom to the milk bottles left by the milkman in the box outside our door. The milk would start to freeze during the winter, causing the cream to rise two or three inches above the bottle. We would scoop the heavy cream right off the top and eat it. This was before milk was homogenized, so the milk and cream separated. The problem for the rest of the family was that this ritual inadvertently left them drinking skim milk. Although it was a blessing in many ways, when we purchased our first refrigerator in 1932, the fun ended because we no longer needed to buy all of our perishable items each day. The job of the iceman disappeared, and we no longer had to empty the drip pan from the ice that melted each day.

The next bit of progress in the area was the opening of the first Big Bear Food Market on Crooks Ave in Paterson, New Jersey. We could not believe so much food was available in one store. People came to the store in droves and walked around like they were visiting a World's Fair. Before the Big Bear Market opened, people would go to the local corner store, stand at the counter, and tell the grocer what they wanted. The grocer would pick out the items, and people never really asked about prices. Most of the time we would put it on our store account and pay it off every week or month. This new shopping concept was a precursor to the supermarket and actually made food shopping a family excursion.

We also witnessed a sad piece of history from our home. Our family was living in Clifton, New Jersey, on May 6, 1937, when we watched the Hindenburg Zeppelin fly over our heads en route to Lakehurst, New Jersey. Less than a half-hour later, the infamous broadcast of the Hindenburg catching on fire and crashing to the ground was heard on the radio.

Telephones were also a great form of entertainment. At the time, people only had one phone in the house. We did not dial the phone number; we would crank the handle and the operator would ask for the number. I actually worked as a phone operator for a short time after high school, earning $14 a week. As an operator, I would connect the four digit phone numbers and keep track of how long people stayed on the line by watching the lights go on and off on the board. To add to the fun, we each had party lines that connected to four homes. We were only supposed to pick up our specific ring (either one, two, three, or four quick rings). Of course everyone would pick up the phone regardless of the number of rings, and we always ended up listening to our neighbor's conversations. The neighbors were always getting upset with us if they caught us listening in.

Our first radio was built from a kit in 1924, and my father assembled it himself. The radios of the day did not have speakers; instead, earphones plugged into the unit. Later, in 1932, my father purchased an RCA Victor Radio with a 78-speed record player for the unheard of amount of $350. The unit was one of the heaviest pieces of furniture in the house. One person could barely move it. The RCA radio had a trumpet amplifier that enabled all of us to sit around and listen to the radio together.

At night we would listen to shows like *Amos and Andy* or *The Shadow Knows* on one of the three stations available. Our favorite nights were those special occasions when we could listen to a boxing match. We would use our imaginations to visualize how badly our favorite fighter was beating up his opponent. Our favorite fights were the Joe Louis bouts. He was the preeminent fighter of my childhood and I can still remember listening to many of his fights.

Before I started high school, my parents sold our summer place. My brother had finished high school and was attending a trade school. I did not want to be alone at the cabin with my mother, so my father thought it was best to sell. My summer escapades were over. I no longer had a chance to see Hans, who by this time had become my first crush. Hans joined the Navy, and my brother went to Casey Jones Aeronautical School in Newark, New Jersey. Both my brother Bill and Hans were always very interested in airplanes. Hans became a pilot, and Bill, an aeronautical engineer. I was left at home, coping with my not-so-happy life with my family.

We moved many times before finally settling in Ridgewood, New Jersey. Mom was against buying a house because she wanted to move every year. I ended up going to six different grade schools (two of them twice) and three different high schools. She finally consented to purchasing a house in Ridgewood in time for my senior year of high school. It was very hard to make friends when I moved this often, so I started to become somewhat of a loner. Fortunately, as fate would have it, I was quite ready to meet someone, and the love of my life was just around the corner…

Chapter 2
COURTSHIP

I met Bill in October of 1940 during our senior year of high school in Ridgewood, New Jersey. Bill was 5 feet 11 inches tall and 180 pounds with dark curly hair and hazel eyes, and he was the only boy in school with a mustache. I was surprised they let him keep his mustache at school. I met Bill through two sisters I became friends with at Ridgewood High – Helen and Chris Simos. I was the new kid on the block, again, and I felt pretty lost. Helen and Chris were in my homeroom class and must have sensed how I felt. Luckily they befriended me right away. They lived about a mile from my home in an apartment above a store on the main street of town. They were from a Greek family with six children, and their parents barely spoke any English.

The family managed a living from the money they made running a small luncheonette called Gus's which consisted of a small counter and about 10 stools. Their saving grace was their location next to the fire department and police station; the men from those departments kept them in business. Helen and Chris worked at the restaurant after school and on Saturdays.

Helen always loved to dance, so we would often practice together during gym glass. I felt she could have been a professional dancer if she had been given the opportunity. Chris had more of a devilish side to her. One of my funniest memories of Chris was watching her run naked through the locker room after gym class and leap over benches just to shock the affluent students in the room. Of course, that consisted of about 75 percent of the Ridgewood population.

Mr. and Mrs. Simos were strict parents from the old country and insisted their children only date Greek boys from the Greek Orthodox church. Helen eventually married a man from the church but it did not last. Chris, on the other hand, snuck out one night to go on a date with my brother. Later, she snuck out for good when she fell in love with an Italian boy from the area and ran away with him to California. After her divorce, Helen also moved to California where she found a very good job at a college in Santa Monica, where she is still actively working with senior citizens. Chris became a registered nurse and had a wonderful life carved out for her and their five children until her husband unexpectedly died at a young age in the late 1950s. She suffers a lot from depression, but with Helen's help, she gets through it. They have traveled together extensively, visiting places throughout Europe and their homeland of the Greek Isles, as well as numerous islands in the Pacific. Bill and I had the chance to see them on several occasions during our travels later in life. Helen, Chris, and I still write letters to each other to this day.

The way I met Bill could have been taken from a scene of a bad romantic movie. After seeing Bill in the hallway while changing classes, I mentioned to Helen that I liked what I saw. A few days later she introduced me to Bill. At the time he was eating an apple and he asked me if I would like a bite. I confidently said no and told him, "I might break your heart if I eat your apple." His reply was, "Eating my apple won't break my heart, but you sure could." Years later, I reminded Bill of our first encounter. He could not believe he said something so corny. I assured him that yes, he did, but he still won me over in that instant.

It did not take long for Bill to ask me if I would like a ride home. I confidently replied that it would be nice, but inside I was thinking, "YES, YES, YES." Bill told me to meet him by the yellow convertible in the parking lot. I waited and waited by this beautiful yellow 1940 convertible Pontiac until he came out, looked at me and said, "Wrong car, follow me." Oops, one of my many blunders. His convertible was out of necessity; his car literally had no top. He had traded his bicycle for the car, which was a wreck of an old Ford Model A, and it was an even trade if that describes the shape of this car. Whenever we drove in the rain or it was cold outside, we held a blanket over us as a roof. Sometimes we would get wet and we were always cold, but the car ran. This old Ford seemed to be apart more than it was together. Bill would take the car apart, find the part he needed at the junkyard for very little money, and proceed to put it back together again. He became so proficient working on Fords that after graduation he worked at Dutch's Mobil Gas Station and fixed all the Fords that came in for repair.

Our class time was mostly spent writing notes to each other rather than listening to the teachers. As soon as the bell rang we would race off to exchange our notes and head to our next class. We did not share any classes, but we did spend our lunchtime together every day. Suddenly I developed this large appetite and asked my mother to pack a larger lunch for me. I would give Bill most of my lunch, saying my mother always packed way too much for me. Sneaky, I know, but all is fair in love and war.

In the 1940s, if a couple went steady, the boy would give the girl his class ring. At this time, even though Bill and I were getting very close, he had not yet given me his ring. Because of this, a fellow I used to roller skate with asked me on a date to a dance in his hometown of Passaic, New Jersey, and I accepted. I knew Jack for about a year and we were just friends. I am not sure how, but Bill found out about our date. Maybe my friend Helen was the instigator. Jack picked me up, but he had to wait because I was not quite ready. When we pulled away from the house, I thought I saw Bill's car down the road, but I was not sure. We were a couple of miles away when Jack's car suddenly broke down. After several tries, it was obvious it was not going to start again. Jack tried jiggling wires and anything else he could think of, but it was to no avail. When I looked down the road, much to my surprise I saw Bill parked on the side of the road. I walked to Bill's car to tell him we were having car problems. With the look of the cat that ate the canary, he grinned and sheepishly replied, "Yes, I know." At that point he whisked me away and we left poor Jack sitting there by the car Bill had sabotaged. I certainly knew it was wrong to do, but it also was one of the most romantic moments of my life. Jack never did get the car to run right. I was not surprised that he never asked me out again.

Shortly after that evening, I received Bill's ring. This meant I was his girl, and it signaled hands off to all other guys. Of course his ring was way too large to wear on my finger so I wore it on a chain around my neck. This also made it easier to hide from my mother. When my friends at school finally received their boyfriends' rings, they tended to show them off in school, especially if they knew another girl had her eyes on their man. People can be cruel, and I am willing to bet almost nothing has changed in how people meet and date since my generation.

Needless to say, my senior year was absolutely useless. As far as education was concerned, it was obvious I had no plans to become a career woman. Quite frankly, I always wanted to be a wife and mother. My father wanted me to go to college and become a dietician. Luckily, he did not force this on me. I think he could sense I preferred to become a stay-at-home mom. In the 1930s, I would guess that approximately 25 percent of women went to college, another 25 percent went straight to work, and 50 percent became stay-at-home mothers as soon as they were married. At the time, it was commonplace for women to stay at home while the husband filled the role of the breadwinner. It was the woman's job to take care of the house and the kids and to make sure the family lived within their means. If we could not afford something, we just forgot about it and did not buy it. People were not bombarded with the opportunities to purchase everything on credit like today.

In order to bring enough money home to help out his mother, Bill had to work several jobs. After school he worked in one of our town gas stations where he pumped gas from 4 p.m. to 9 p.m. He would then sleep from 10 p.m. to 3 a.m. and wake up to work again from 3 a.m. to 6 a.m. with a milkman, running bottles from the truck to the homes in the neighborhood. As if that was not enough, on Saturday nights he cleaned the ovens in the Ridgewood Bakery. On Saturdays, Bill spent the afternoon playing football. He was a lineman and co-captain of the high school football team. I was very proud of Bill. Even with his busy schedule, Bill still managed to keep his grades up.

We were allowed to go out on dates on Wednesday and Friday nights and all day on Sunday. We chose Wednesday and Friday nights because they were the only evenings he could convince someone else to work for him at the gas station. I always had to be home by 10:30 p.m. which seemed very early to me. We could not go out on Saturday nights since Bill cleaned the bakery ovens, so I would spend those evenings primarily trying to appease my mother so she would let me continue to see Bill. She did not like the fact that I was dating, and she certainly had no idea I was in possession of Bill's ring. Of course it did not help matters when my brother playfully pointed out to my parents that I had a hickey on my neck. My mother gave out an exasperated, "Well!" and it was all my father could do to keep a straight face at that moment.

We spent many of our Wednesday nights sitting together at The Corner Shop, which was a local ice cream parlor located across the street from Bill's apartment. The store had a small counter with eight stools and was run by a nice Italian man named Al Merchio. He always enjoyed seeing Bill and I together. He used to tease us about being lovesick kids. Our favorite treat was a root beer float with chocolate ice cream, which at the time cost a quarter. Of course, many times out of necessity we had to split our drink, but one of the most romantic moments in a young person's life is sharing an ice cream soda with your first love.

Another one of our favorite hangouts was located in Patterson, New Jersey, about four miles from our home. It was a hot dog stand called Johnny & Hanges, which was a gold mine in the area. The place was known for having its own special recipe for chilidogs. They became successful selling their secret sauce on the East Coast, and the next generation of their family still runs the business today.

We would sit in the car and eat 25 cent hot dogs and drink 10 cent coffee. I used to love the raw onion on the hot dogs, but if I was planning to sneak a kiss or two at the end of the night, that was not such a bright idea. Our evenings were spent getting to know each other, our dreams, our family plans (at the time Bill wanted 10 children), and most importantly, our feelings for each other. From time to time we would be interrupted by some of Bill's friends who saw his car in the parking lot. Bill would quickly shoo them away because our time was limited since I had to be home by 10:30 p.m.

On Friday nights we used to go to the movies. Bill's sister Helen was the cashier at the movie theatre, so we would get in for free. If we hurried, after the movie, we could park in front of my house for a little while before I had to go inside. This used to annoy my mother to no end. I could rest assured that promptly at 10:30 p.m. the front porch light would be flicked on and off, which was my queue that the date was over. I was never ready to come in, but I did not want to make any waves with my mother. She had expected me to date someone a little more "upper crust," so I did not push my limits with her.

Oh, Sunday wonderful Sunday. We were able to spend the whole day together. My mother would fix us a picnic basket with a baked chicken, hard-boiled eggs, pickles, fruit, and cookies. It was always a really nice feast, but I never really understood why she would go to such great lengths to please us. I always felt my father had something to do with it because he saw Bill as such a hard worker and gave him a lot of credit. Of course it would have been more romantic if I would have tried to make our picnic by myself, but at the time I could not boil water. The kitchen had always been out of bounds for me. Mom wanted to talk more about the latest fashions and hairstyles or help her change her hair.

The picnic basket always included a cold roasted chicken. It was not until many years later that Bill told me the only meat provided to welfare recipients was chicken. He ate so much chicken that he never wanted to see chicken again. And what do I pack on our romantic picnic, chicken.

We usually went to Bear Mountain State Park in New York for our Sunday dates. It is a beautiful park close to the Hudson River, about 45 miles from our home. We would take the lake drive through the park that took us past seven lakes. We would pick a different spot each time – one lake for swimming, one for camping, and others for boating and fishing. During the winter, ice skaters could be seen on every single lake. At the end of the lake drive was Bear Mountain Inn. The inn had a cafeteria with a big stone fireplace where everyone would gather around after swimming in the summer or skiing and skating in the winter.

The state park did not have an entrance fee, so during the summer we would swim in the lakes, hike in the woods, play shuffleboard, or take a walk on the bridge that hung above an enclosed area containing bears. Even during the winter the mountain had a small ski slope that was free of charge, but we had to walk up the hill because they did not have a ski lift. Farther into the park was a small amusement center with bumper cars, a merry-go-round, and the whip. We had such wonderful Sundays there. Later in life, we took our children back whenever possible, and they enjoyed it just as much.

On my seventeenth birthday, Bill surprised me with a maple hope chest. It is unfortunate that this tradition died through the years. I always thought it was a great way to start planning our life together. At the time, a hope chest meant that an engagement ring was on the way. A hope chest typically measured approximately 5 feet long, 3 feet wide, and 2 feet high, and it opened from the top. The chests were usually lined with cedar to prevent moth infestation. The objective was to fill the chest with all of the items you hoped you would need in the future to start a family. We had wonderful memories of filling up our hope chest. I filled it with linens, blankets, dishes, pots, pans, and silverware. I also made many items that I placed in the chest such as crochet doilies, afghans, and a green smoking jacket that waited for Bill's return. To go with the smoking jacket, I put in a blue negligee for me. Bill gave me the chest in early 1941 and I had it filled up by the time he returned home from World War II.

The delight of the hope chest was squelched by my mother, who was sitting in the front room, speechless, waiting for me to come home from school. Until then, she had not realized how serious Bill and I were about each other. I guess my mother thought I would stay home with her forever, so this was quite a shock for her. She was very cold towards the idea, but I did not care. I was too excited about what this gift meant for our relationship. Since the cat was out of the bag, I was no longer worried about wearing Bill's class ring in front of my mother since a ring paled in comparison to the significance of the hope chest.

With the addition of the hope chest to our lives, our Friday night dates took on a new meaning. We now spent Friday nights playing quarter bingo at the Elk's Club. The prizes were merchandise instead of money, and they were items we would need for the house. We would jump for joy when we won a set of towels or a bed sheet. We did not care what we won because we needed everything. We placed every item we won into the hope chest among our growing treasures.

One Sunday Bill picked me up and said we were going on a cruise. "When, where, how?" I asked. "Never mind, you will see when we get there," Bill replied. We drove to the New Jersey side of the Hudson River in Hoboken and paid a nickel to ride on the ferry to New York City. The trip took about 20 minutes. Instead of disembarking in New York, we remained on the ferry and rode back and forth for most of the day on the same nickel. We watched a man walk around the boat playing an accordion, hoping for a handout. The boat also had vendors selling hot peanuts and roasted chestnuts. What could be better than spending a romantic day on the water with the person I loved, eating hot peanuts and listening to music? It is a bygone era, and I cannot imagine that kids have the same kind of experiences today.

After our cruise, I decided it was my turn to create a romantic evening. I don't know what I was thinking, but one evening when my parents were out for the night, I invited Bill over for a home-cooked meal. I knew this was going to be an issue because I was never introduced to housewife fundamentals, and I barely knew how to boil water. It sounded easy enough – a dinner of pork chops, potatoes, canned peas, and applesauce. The first problem hit when I wanted to start peeling potatoes and realized we had none in the house. I called Bill and told him my problem. He solved the issue by bringing the potatoes with him. The potatoes were good, and the applesauce tasted fine because it came straight out of a can, but the peas were cooked right out of their skins and the poor pork chops were like burnt toast. If Bill was not going to ask for his class ring back that night, I figured I had nothing to worry about because it could not get much worse.

We graduated from high school in June of 1941. We did not go to our graduation prom for several reasons, primarily the cost, but Bill also had a desire to stay as far away from a dance floor as possible. Instead, we saved our money together for about five months to join Bill's mother's lodge on a bus trip to Coney Island. Coney Island is on the southern tip of Brooklyn, and the people living in New York City would flock there in the summer for the swimming and the amusement park. With all of the people sitting on the sand, we could hardly see the actual beach, just people as far as the eye could see. The park had six roller coasters and we rode each one as well as a new parachute ride. Normally I was a conservative merry-go-round type of person, but it was hard to explain how I felt that day. I just felt so safe with Bill that there was no limit to what I was willing to try. We ate one junk food after another all day long. The best part of the day was the long bus ride home. Bill's arm was around me the entire time, and we continually stole kisses from each other when we thought no one was watching.

In the fall of 1941 Bill and I were engaged. My parents knew nothing about it because I wanted it to be a special for us, and not turn into another fight with my mother. We went out to celebrate with a large group of our friends at Frank Daily's Meadowbrook, a night club in Montclair, New Jersey. The cover charge was $3 per person, and we sat around all night drinking one Coke. I remember the place had a very small dance floor, but it did not matter because most of the people just went to listen to the big band sound. There were usually so many musicians in these bands that they took up most of the stage. It was such a thrill to listen to performers such as Benny Goodman, Artie Shaw, and Harry James. On the night of our engagement party, Tommy Dorsey was playing, and a young man came out to perform. He was so skinny he barley filled out his suit, but he could really sing. We listened to him perform songs such as "Come Fly With Me," "It Had to Be You," "This Love of Mine," "What is This Thing Called Love," and "Try A Little Tenderness." When the announcer said, "Give Frank Sinatra a big hand folks," we gave him a standing ovation. It may have been his first of many. We left the club thinking this guy could really turn into quite a performer some day. When he became famous, I always enjoyed telling people that Frank Sinatra sang at my engagement party.

After graduation, Bill worked full time at the gas station making $18 a week, or 45 cents an hour. He could see no reason why we could not get married on that income, but I felt it was not quite enough for the two of us to live on. At the time, the average salary was $2,050 a year, or just under $1 per hour, and the minimum wage was 30 cents an hour. This meant that our income was halfway between average and poor. By mutual agreement, we decided I was to be a stay-at-home

Mom and he would be the breadwinner. Unfortunately, we could not adhere to this arrangement until the end of World War II.

Bill's proposal to me was very different. He didn't ask me to marry him, he asked me if I "would I be willing to be with him the rest of my life and face together whatever life throws at us." I said, "Yes, because all I ask is for you to love me forever the way you do now." "That's easy," he replied. It was easy for both of us.

While Bill worked at the gas station, I worked around the block from him as a receptionist for a podiatrist. I had a terrific boss, and every time Bill passed my office getting parts or testing a car, he would play a tune on his horn. Even though the doctor was working on a patient, he always commented, "There he is." We kept these jobs for the first year after high school graduation.

Although we were typical teenagers who really did not pay attention to current events, history now shows how rapidly the world was changing between 1939 and 1941. We were kids with more important things on our minds, like dating. Germany had already started its campaign across Europe, but it never really came up as a topic of conversation. None of us realized that Japan was building up its military and starting to aggressively pursue its doctrine throughout the South Pacific. Of course, all of that would change less than six months after we graduated from high school.

Sixty years before September 11, 2001, I lived through a similar moment that defined our generation. However, unlike 2001, we received the first reports in the afternoon and over the radio. At the time, I don't think most people even knew the United States had a military outpost in Hawaii, let alone that it was in Pearl Harbor. The bombing took place on Sunday morning in Hawaii, however with the time change (Hawaii is five hours earlier than New Jersey) and the lag time in news reports of the day, it was mid-afternoon on the east coast before the story first broke. For everyone in the country, our lives suddenly changed on December 7, 1941. Before that day, we were all carefree teenagers. In an instant, we all became adults and patriots.

The next day men started lining up to enlist in the armed forces. I knew Bill would soon join them, but I asked him to please stay with me as long as he could. A remarkable feeling of patriotism enveloped the country overnight, fueling the rapid expansion of the war effort. Bill took a job with Wrights Aeronautical, a company that manufactured airplane propellers. To my delight, this kept him from joining the war for about 10 months. This was also the first time Bill ever had some extra money in his pocket, as he was now making $40 a week at the plant. Bill used some of the extra money to purchase a used Indian Motorcycle from the Ridgewood police department; they were selling off their old bikes when new models arrived.

As the war expanded overseas, people on the home front did the best they could to help the cause. I can honestly say I never heard people complain about the rationing of food and materials. Try to picture being forced to ration gas in today's world to the point where you only had enough to get back and forth to work. We could only have meat once a week, and we were only allowed to buy a pound of butter if we returned a pound's worth of grease from the food we cooked. The grease was then converted into lubricants by the military. People plowed their backyards and grew victory gardens. For most people, the only way to supplement food rations was to plant a garden of their own. We knitted caps, gloves, hats, and scarves, and donated them to the Red Cross.

Trains were limited to military use, so people did not travel. Industries were converted to provide supplies and materials to assist with wartime needs. Automobile manufacturers such as Ford and General Motors produced jeeps, tanks, and military vehicles. My father's mill converted from the custom fabrics to uniform cloth. Ammunition plants sprung up out of nowhere, and all of the shipyards were working overtime.

When our neighbors started leaving for the war, there loved ones waited for the mailman every day hoping to hear some good news. Every home with a family member in the service feared seeing the Western Union man delivering a telegram about the loss of their son. Everyone with a son serving in the military hung a navy blue cloth banner with red trim and a white star in the center in their window. Households had one banner for each member in the military. If there was a gold star on the banner, it unfortunately meant that their son had been killed in action.

Between the work Bill was doing at Wrights and my perseverance, I was able to keep Bill from enlisting until November of 1942. By then he told me he simply had to go because he could not face the thought of this friends enlisting while he stayed behind. Bill drove alone to Patterson, New Jersey where the armed services used a formerly vacant office building as a recruiting station. Being a typical young and impatient male, when Bill looked at the long lines for both the Army and Navy, he chose the shortest line so he could get through the quickest. This is how he became a Marine. At the time, he did not realize why the line to sign up for the Marine Corps was so short. Every man who served in the military was a hero, no matter which branch they chose.

I asked Bill to take the longest grace period available before shipping out for basic training. He agreed and was allowed to stay home for only 30 days. During that time, we considered getting married, but Bill was leery about the idea. He could not be certain of the condition he would be in when he returned from the war, if he returned at all. I did not agree with the decision but I conceded, so we decided to wait until the war was over.

My mother let me see Bill every day, but she really had no choice in the matter. Although the countdown was always playing in the back of our minds, neither one of us tried to show it. I immediately quit my job so we could spend every possible moment together. We made the most of our 30-day reprieve. Bill used some of the extra money he made to buy his first new suit along with an overcoat and fedora, and he wore it the day he took me to Radio City Music Hall. We decided to spend a day with his three nieces and took them for a pony ride. We spent time going back to Bear Mountain (and necking), and on another day, we toured New York City (and did some more necking). We went back to our favorite hangouts like Johnny & Hanges for hot dogs (and necking) or The Corner Shop for ice cream (and necking).

When Bill enlisted, I went to work at another Wright's Defense Plant in Woodridge, New Jersey, where I learned to weld airplane engines. It was easy to get a job because just about every plant was geared up for the war effort and constantly hiring. By 1942, much of the manufacturing work was being handled by women because the men were going off to fight. We switched shifts every week, from 8 a.m. to 4 p.m., then 4 p.m. to midnight, then midnight to 8 a.m. I have no idea why they changed our shifts like this, but at the time, everyone had a "Proud to be an American" feeling that caused us not to question anything.

From 1941 to 1945, more than 16 million Americans served in the armed forces. On November 24, 1942, our 30 days were up, and Bill became part of that number. I drove Bill to the train station in Ridgewood and we said our goodbyes. I watched the train pull away as I stood alone on the platform and it ripped my heart out. There was no way to be certain what was going to happen in the future or where he would be stationed. It is so hard to convey the feeling of helplessness I felt, having absolutely no control over the path our lives were about to take. No wishing, begging, pleading, or praying was going to bring Bill back home until the war was over, if at all. I cried so hard driving home that when I reached our driveway I rammed into the center post of our garage door because I could not see it through the tears.

Little did I know that we would be together again in three months.

This chapter is dedicated to the more than 300,000 American men and women who died during World War II. My thoughts and prayers are always with you and your families.

Chapter 3
MARRIAGE

After Bill enlisted, he felt it would be best to wait until the war was over before getting married. Many men were concerned that they might come home as invalids and burden their wives, or not return at all, leaving behind widows and possibly children. Although I would have married Bill at any moment, we decided in the end it was best to wait.

When his 30-day leave was up, Bill hopped on a train for boot camp at Camp Lejeune, North Carolina, on Parris Island, where he became one of the 142,000 people that joined the Marines in 1942. At the time, the Marines did not even pay for train fare to get to the training facility. Basic training was unbelievably rough, which was not a surprise after learning what the Marines must face in war. Bill did not have much time for writing, but when he did, I felt so badly about what he was going through. His sergeant told them that they would be trained to kill anyone or anything by the time they left in three months. It's not a wonder that some of the men were never the same after basic training or the war. I am sure this type of training was necessary to give soldiers a fighting chance of survival, but it clearly personified the old adage that war is hell.

Boot camp lasted three months. The Marines did not have a graduation ceremony, and visitors were not allowed. After basic training, Bill was sent to an aeronautical school in Jacksonville, Florida. He applied for bombardier training but could not pass the physical because of a punctured eardrum, an injury that would have caused him too much trouble flying at high altitudes. He was disappointed, but in my mind this might have saved his life. He instead became an aeronautical mechanic and was transferred to Jacksonville Naval Air Station in Florida for training, where he would spend the next six months.

When I received the news in March of 1943 that Bill would be stationed in one place for six months, I abandoned the idea of waiting until the war was over before getting married. I quit my job, packed a suitcase, and sent Bill a telegram saying, "Arriving by Greyhound on Friday at 3 p.m. Meet me at the terminal." I left on a Tuesday and arrived in Jacksonville on Friday. I expected Bill to be waiting for me with his arms wide open. Of course, this was based on my assumptions that Bill received my telegram and that the Maine Corps would not have an issue with Bill leaving base to pick up his girlfriend.

This was my first of many blunders regarding the Marines and the way that they operate. In my naivety, I just assumed Bill could tell his sergeant that he needed to go to town to meet his girl at the bus terminal. Yeah, right. Three days later, I was still sitting in the terminal waiting for my husband-to-be. I was afraid to leave in case I missed him, so I just ate candy bars from a vending machine and slept on a bench in the terminal each night. I later tried to think of another solution, like going to the base to find him, but I convinced myself that at the moment I left the bus station, Bill would show up. I was 19 years old and I had never been away from home on my own before, but I was starting to learn very fast. During the three days I spent at the station, not one employee checked on me or asked me why I was sitting alone and had not left the building.

Finally, on the third day, Bill was able to catch a bus from the base and take the 10-mile ride into town to the station. I was walking around the terminal, and Bill came up from behind me and said, "Are you looking for someone?" I nearly fell over in a state of shock from seeing him. He looked so handsome dressed in his Marine uniform. My only concern was how skinny he looked; he had dropped more than 40 pounds since the time he left. However, he now walked very erect and confidently. I was so impressed and proud of my future husband. He would stop and salute every officer that passed. Since this was a town of 15,000 servicemen, the salutes were frequent. I must say his last salute of the day was always as sharp and crisp as his first in the morning.

We walked to the closest place to eat, which was Morrison's cafeteria, and loaded our table with food, but we were both so excited to see each other that we could hardly eat anything. I told Bill that I came to Florida to get married and be with him while he went to school for the next six months. He was thrilled with the idea. We found a place for me to stay. It was a dinky hotel called St. Albans that cost $14 a week. It was so dirty that I ended up cleaning my own room. In the 1940s, it was unheard of to live together unless you were married. In our case, I am not saying there was not any hanky-panky going on, but given the times, we were not living together.

By evening Bill had to be back at the base. Of the 15,000 servicemen in the area, the vast majority were sailors. Since I was still pretty young and naïve about the world, Bill gave me strict orders to stay inside after dark. He explained to me that he would not be able to come back to town again until the following Sunday. I spent my time idling away. I sat in the lobby of the hotel where I did not feel as lonesome as I did in my room. All I could do was think about ways to afford to stay in Florida near Bill. I knew I had to quickly figure things out because my money was dwindling fast. My first move was to find less expensive lodging. Then, I needed to find a job.

Bill arrived as promised on Sunday. He had to let me know how hard it was to get permission from the captain to leave and get married. The war was young, and the service was not used to wives following their husbands. That was fine because were not used to having the military tell us what we could do either. How soon we both learned that lesson.

On Sunday we went to the Presbyterian Church to see the minister about marrying us. I asked the minister to please open the church doors in case someone wanted to come in and watch. In addition, I requested that we both walk down the isle while the organist played the wedding march.

I had a very busy week before our wedding. I went to Cohen's Department Store, a very large store in Jacksonville, to apply for a job. I went upstairs to the office and met the store manager. There was an elderly gentleman sitting in a very comfortable chair who seemed to be half-listening to the conversation. I pleaded my case to the manager, telling him that I would only be in town for six months while my husband was in school at the base. I told him the only way I could manage to stay was to get a job to pay for my room and board. The manager did not respond for what seemed like an eternity. Much to my surprise, the elderly gentleman, who happened to be the owner, said, "Give her a job." This was my first big break.

I worked as a salesgirl in the men's department with another woman and two men. I started work the next day. While working, I asked around to see if anyone at the store knew of any rooms for rent because the hotel was more than I could afford. One of my colleagues, Mr. Fletcher, lived just two blocks from the store. He also owned the house next door to his, which he converted into small apartments and rooms. He explained to me that the only room he had available was up in the attic, but he would be willing to rent it to me for only $10 a week. I took it sight unseen and moved in that evening. It had a bed, dresser, and clothes closet, with dark brown woodwork and tan walls. I was on the third floor, and the community bathroom was on the second floor. In March and April, it was gloomy but bearable. When the weather warmed up in late spring and summer, it was like an oven in the room. When I woke in the morning, my hair would be as wet as if I held it under a faucet.

Living in this area was quite awkward for me. It was as if the Civil War never ended. Because I was from the North, the Southerners would not even acknowledge my existence. The Southern girls would sit on the front porch and gossip during the day. They never once spoke to me or invited me to sit down. I just told myself to hang tough and that no matter what happened, we would be leaving as soon as Bill's training was completed.

We were to be married the following Saturday on March 21, 1943. Bill's captain surprised him with a weekend liberty. We had decided it would be easiest to meet at the church. I bought a navy blue dress with white polka dots to wear for our ceremony. It was very inexpensive, but I wanted to wear something new. I brought very little with me to Jacksonville: just three dresses, a skirt, and two blouses. When we both arrived at the church, we went into the minister's office, and he said, "Follow me." We went through the side door, walked into the church, and stood in front of the altar. The doors were still closed in the back as the minister pulled out a piece of paper and began to read from it. At first I thought we were having a rehearsal since we had not walked down the aisle and music was not playing as we discussed with the minister the previous weekend. He also forgot to put Bill's hand in mine to receive his ring even though I received mine. Although it did not go as planned, I quickly wised up to the situation. To repay the favor, the envelope we brought as a donation for the ceremony was mysteriously empty as we left the church.

It was pouring rain when we got out of the church. They say it's good luck to have rain on your wedding, and I believe it is. I told Bill I moved out of the hotel so we had a little further to walk. I guess the new dress I bought was a little too cheap or it just did not like rain because it started shrinking very fast. With every step, it went an inch higher. By the time we reached the house, I was wearing a mini-dress, long before fashion designers had thought of them. Bill thought I looked really cool, and I felt pretty cool with the dress hardly covering me. I guess I should have spent a little more money on what turned out to be my wedding gown, but my money needed to afford my stay in Florida. I had already sold my roller skates and my receptionist's uniform to buy my bus ticket to Florida, and I was not going to ask my parents for money. I had made the decision to go to Florida on my own, so it was up to me.

We finally reached my new place. We walked up the stairs to my new room. Bill just accepted the room for what it was, but I think he had other thoughts on his mind. We bought a can of grapefruit juice and paper cups and toasted to each other, then I asked him if he was sure we were married after that botched up ceremony. He assured me that the license read husband and wife. I think that scared him for a second. Have no fear; our one-night honeymoon commenced immediately.

Chapter 4
MILITARY TRAINING AND WORLD WAR II

Now that we were married, it was time to try and settle into our new life together. However, our life together consisted of a few random weekend leaves. Financially, we were really making headway. Bill's military pay was $25 a month, and I was making $14 a week at Cohen's. I still had about $20 left out of the $30 I brought with me from New Jersey. As soon as I received my paycheck, I immediately paid $10 a week for rent and an additional 50 cents per week to wash my clothes in the bathroom sink, located one floor below in the community bathroom. I actually did all of my laundry in that sink and hung it up in my room. I had $3.50 left each week for food, which was not much for a person with a big appetite. I bought a loaf of bread and a jar of jelly to cover both my breakfast and lunch, and I ate supper at Morrison's Cafeteria where I could get a bowl of chili, macaroni and cheese, or soup for 15 cents. I always had a bag of apples in my room to help out when I got hungry. I had to keep food hidden in my suitcase because we were not allowed to eat in our rooms. Bill's pay was used for cigarettes and to take us out to eat when he was on overnight liberty.

Much to my chagrin, here I was thinking that I made at least some of the rules about our marriage. How wrong I was in underestimating the constraints of the military. During our six months in Jacksonville, we only had six weekends together as well as every other Sunday. This was not what I had in mind. I was terribly lonesome all week, but it was worth it when Bill was able to see me on liberty.

Unlike boot camp, Bill had a graduation ceremony after finishing his aeronautical mechanics training. On August 1, 1943, I was able to visit the base to see him graduate. I was so proud watching him march so erectly and looking so handsome in his Marine uniform alongside his fellow soldiers in the Marine Aviation Separation Unit One, MCAB.

Soon after graduation, Bill was assigned to a base in Cherry Point, North Carolina. I packed my one suitcase, into which I now added a clock and an iron, and headed for the bus station. The contents of the suitcase increased with each move and became heavier to carry around. The trip to North Carolina was about a day's ride from Jacksonville by bus. The bus arrived in the town of Beaufort, North Carolina, a small village on the Atlantic coast. The town was as close as I could get to the base, but Cherry Point was still about 10 miles away. Since I left before Bill, I planned to leave my new address with the postmaster at the local post office. This way, Bill could find out where I was staying when he arrived a few days later. This seemed like a great method because every town had a local post office, but unfortunately, the postmaster was very reluctant to give my address to a total stranger – even one serving in the armed forces during the war. We would need to come up with another idea if and when we moved again.

Bill's assignment in Cherry Point was a dream come true for both of us because he was able to come home every night. We were now actually living like a married couple, and it felt like we were in paradise. Beaufort was a small fishing town whose shoreline housed a general store, a fish house where boats unloaded their catches, and a tiny movie theatre with only a couple of benches that featured 10-cent shows. The town was so small that there was not a restaurant of any kind in the area.

All work in Beaufort was centered on the fishing industry. Literally, everyone either worked in the fish house or on a boat. The town only had two streets, neither of which was paved. The first street in town was Main Street, and it was lined with no more than 20 houses running up and down both sides. There was also a dirt lane called Turkey Lane where the poorest white and black people lived. When I walked down Turkey Lane, I did not think twice about starting up a conversation with one of the black women on the street, however it appeared to make many of them extremely uncomfortable. Again, I had forgotten that I was a Northerner living in the South, and this was not how things worked in 1943.

Once again, I found myself wondering how I was ever going to find a place to live in such a little town. The owner of the fish house had a very old but large home, so it seemed like a good place to start. Throughout my travels, I truly felt that my guardian angel was really working overtime. The lady of the house, Rosalie, was very young. In fact, she was just six years older than me. I could tell instantly that she was lonesome. Her husband was out on the fishing boats most of the time, and rumor had it that he liked to visit Turkey Lane for some extracurricular activity. Rosalie was more than willing to have company, so it was not terribly hard to talk my way into one of her extra bedrooms. As a bonus, she gave me the front bedroom so I would have an ocean view – all for $5 a week.

I was living in this small town with a population of next to nothing, and everything smelled like day-old fish. I had no chance of getting a job, no place to eat, and the ever-popular problem: I had no money. My only choice was to sit on the porch and hope for a handout. Bill lived with me at the house instead of at the base. He reported to the base before breakfast and came home after dinner, so his meals were covered, but my living arrangement did not include meals.

Luckily, Rosalie needed company as much as I needed food, so when she went into the kitchen to eat she invited me along. What a surprise mealtime was. Every afternoon we deep-fried a batch of fish and heaped it onto a plate. Sometimes Rosalie had shrimp, but most of the time it was mullet, pronounced "m-u-u-u-let" (heavy on the "mul" – really drawing it out, followed by a short "et"). For a side dish, we always had a bowl of stewed pears, pronounced "Pars" in this area. When we got hungry, we simply grabbed a hunk of fish in one hand while we spooned a pear into our mouths with the other. As they would say in Beaufort, "We done et." So this is how I lived and ate while living in Beaufort, North Carolina.

I really enjoyed this little town and the people that lived there. Bill had a harder time because he did not care for fish, and he was hard-pressed to find an area of town where he could not smell it. In exchange for food, I used to fascinate Rosalie with stories about my trips to New York City. Rosalie would sit on the porch listening with her mouth wide open, gawking at me as I tried to explain the concept of a subway train to her. She could not understand how a train could run underground right through all that dirt. I had to explain the whole concept of tunnels, elevators, escalators, and skyscrapers to her. Of course, I was just as fascinated hearing about her childhood on Harkers Island. The ferry was the only way on or off the island, and it went once a week to the mainland, which was Beaufort.

I will always be thankful for the knowledge I received from all of the different types of people I met along the way. This was information I could never find on my own or read in a book. It was truly an adventure to see how people lived across this country. If I could ever give others a single piece of advice, it would be not to read it, but to live it.

Although I was fascinated with Beaufort, we did not live there for more than a few months. Part of being in the Marine Corps during the war meant a life of constant transfers. In some ways it was just as well because I was getting a little tired of eating fish and pears every day. By now I had met many of Bill's friends as well as his sergeant. Getting to know the sergeant was extremely helpful because he would let us know a week ahead of time when the unit was being transferred to a new base. This gave me a head start to the next town, providing me a better opportunity to find a new place to live. Strange as it may seem, we were having a great time. Most importantly, we were together. I just could not have imagined staying in New Jersey waiting for Bill to come home. No matter what, nothing was going to keep me away, and I guess Bill had already figured that out about me.

In October of 1943, our next move was farther north and east to the tip of the state in Atlantic, North Carolina. Atlantic was a small peninsula jutting into the Atlantic Ocean. As I was riding there on the bus, little did I know that compared to Atlantic, Beaufort would feel like the big city I left behind. No other wife went to Atlantic, which really should have told me something. It should have been my first clue when Bill told me it would be easy to find him because of the size of the town. The Marine base was actually nothing more than a crude air strip surrounded by small makeshift buildings. Only a handful of personnel were stationed in the area. The Marine presence was due to rumors that a German sub was spotted off the coast. This was now an area that needed to be patrolled around the clock so the base suddenly needed planes, pilots, and mechanics.

I was a Jersey girl who kept finding herself moving deeper and deeper into the boondocks of the Atlantic Coast. Atlantic was not even considered a town; it was merely a field with approximately eight houses scattered helter-skelter with a path connecting one to the other. I never saw the residents of these houses walking around town. The few local residents in the area kept to themselves. At the end of the row sat a small country store. The store was located on the only paved road, which led out of town. The backdrop to the store was the Atlantic Ocean situated on a rocky shoreline. The store was so small it did not even have electricity. It sold limited hardware supplies such as nails and shovels as well as grocery staples and canned goods.

I never remember seeing any children in area. In fact, I hardly remember seeing anyone except the storekeeper and the truck driver, who delivered food each week from the only large town in the area, Morehead City, which was located about 30 miles away.

When I arrived in town, the bus stopped in front of the store. Clearly this was going to be the only place Bill could come to find me. I think he knew this ahead of time but did not want to spoil the surprise. As soon as I arrived, I told the storeowner my plight about needing a place to stay. Morehead City was the only place in the area with apartments for rent, but it was more of a recreational area where people went to the beach for the day, and I knew I could not afford to live there. It was also quite a distance from the base where Bill was stationed. Luckily the shopkeeper had the inside scoop on the only vacant place to live in Atlantic. It was a house a little ways in the woods and in desperate need of repair – but it was vacant. Oh, and there was another tiny bit of information about the house: it was abandoned and rumored to be haunted. The people who lived in the area swore that they saw balls of fire rolling out of the door every so often, but I was welcome to live there if I dared. I asked the gentleman who I should see about renting the house, but no one knew who actually owned the place. To me, that meant one thing: I could live there rent-free.

When I saw the house, I realized how far away from New Jersey I now was living. However, we had the chance to live in an entire house instead of a single room. In actuality, it was "most" of a house. It had a front and back door, as well as a porch that connected on two sides. However, all of the paint had worn off from the harsh salt winds coming off the ocean. The steps were rickety and glass was missing from many of the windows, but it was home. Lord only knows how long this house sat empty.

Inside the house, we had a front room that still had a usable potbelly stove. Bill brought home wooden orange crates from the base that we used as our front room furniture. Ironically, the bedroom still contained an old bed. In the kitchen there was a hand pump for water that normally worked except on the occasions when I would forget to leave a cup of water for priming it in the morning. This would leave me pumping my head off before I could draw any water. Whoever last lived in the house must have left in a hurry because they left behind other helpful items such as a kerosene stove that we cooked on every night and a flatiron to take care of Bill's uniform. We also found an old washtub out in the woods along with a pail for carrying wood from the forest. The house did not have indoor plumbing. Instead, we had an outhouse down the path a way, and it was Bill's job to get it into usable condition.

Bill brought home blankets and cardboard to cover up the windows. Luckily, I was kind of adopted by Bill's unit. Whenever I needed something, one of the guys would always find a way to come up with some used items from the base. This is how we obtained forks, knives, cups, and plates. I purchased a coffee pot and frying pan from the store to complete our cookware. With all this stuff in our own home, I guess I thought I was now ready to become a housewife. Once again, I had no idea how much I still had to learn. Learning to use the flatiron on Bill's uniforms was a skill in its own right. The military frowned upon burnt flatiron mark on shirts.

I would venture to the store on Saturday mornings when the truck came to town, but it did not mean there were more choices available. My first shopping experience was a rude awakening. I arrived and was told that the truck had chicken today. "Great," I thought, "I could make one for dinner." Much to my surprise, he didn't hand me a nice packaged chicken ready to cook, but instead he dropped a live chicken into my hands. I spent the next few minutes walking back to the house gingerly holding onto the chicken by its feet. The entire way home the bird was dangling upside down a few feet from the ground, squawking its head off. I am not sure which one of us was more surprised by the predicament.

I was laughing to myself thinking about the surprise I had for Bill. I figured I had just acquired a pet so I shoved my friend under the washtub outside and waited for further instructions. We had to wait until the following day for Bill to get an axe. He told me to make boiling water while he chopped the head off because he knew we had to dip the chicken into hot water to remove the feathers. I put water in the washtub, and it took forever to heat up. I think we were supposed to just dip the chicken, but we let him soak for awhile in the hot water, sans head. Unfortunately, not only the feathers came off of the bird, but skin and other parts fell off as well. But we had chicken. I think it was really brave of Bill to eat with me instead of eating at the base, however he always looked first to see if the washtub was on the ground when he walked through the door, just to be safe.

Our washtub also doubled as our bathtub. This worked very well until Bill decided to take a bath with me. We had to tangle up together then try and sit down. When we finally got settled down into the water, we would realize that most of it had already run out of the tub. This would have been an issue in a normal house, but there was no need to worry here. The water ran right from the open floor planks to the ground. Since we were without proper plumbing, we inadvertently created our own drainage system.

By early December, there was a pretty good chill in the air and we had to start thinking about heat. On one side of the house we noticed a few pieces of coal. Evidently, someone had dumped coal there for years. By digging into the ground a little ways we found enough coal to create a nice little pile. After awhile the coal supply depleted so we decided to convert to wood. Unfortunately for the house, the best supply of wood was the side porch. It carried us as long as we needed heat, but by the time we left Atlantic, the porch had been reduced to only the front side. We never kept the potbelly going during the night because we were afraid it would burn the house down while we were asleep. With cardboard bedroom windows it was also necessary to get dressed before going to bed. That bedroom felt like a refrigerator by morning.

It was now December of 1943 and a big event was drawing near for us – our first Christmas as man and wife. I found a little pine tree in the woods that I placed in a can of dirt. Next I made some paper ornaments and put a candle next to the tree. I gave Bill a pair of socks from the store, and he gave me a candy bar and lots of hugs and kisses. Mostly, we just felt lucky enough to still be together. Bill had not been sent overseas, and we were celebrating Christmas as a couple instead of via letter from overseas. Neither one of us could have asked for anything more.

After the holidays Bill was transferred to Kinston, North Carolina, which was fortunately only about an hour away by bus. This time I left a week before Bill to get a head start on living arrangements. When I packed our large suitcase this time, I added a coffee pot, frying pan, a couple of plates, cups, and utensils. Bill's friend asked if I would meet up with his wife Martha from Chicago and help her find a room in Kinston. Never again! Kinston is a fairly big city, and she decided she wanted to live in a better section of town that would likely be more than my budget would allow. Nevertheless, we went to look. During the war, most people rented their spare rooms to wives and girlfriends who came down to visit their sweethearts. When we went into the best part of town, the owners asked if our husbands were officers, which kind of pissed me off.

We found a place with two bedrooms, which the woman rented to us with some hesitation. On our third day there, Martha asked if I had an iron, which I did. Soon there was a knock on my door and she sheepishly said, "Mina, look what I did." She had placed a sheet on the floor to use as an ironing board for her dress, and she burned a spot right into the rug. On the fourth day, we were kicked out. No wonder they only wanted to rent to officers' wives. I told Martha she was on her own, and I headed for the other side of town. She stayed in a hotel for a little while and then headed back to Chicago.

Since retrieving my address at the local post office did not work in other towns, we decided to leave my information for Bill at the USO building in each town. The USO, or United Service Organizations, was always willing to help out servicemen and their wives in any way they could. Each USO was usually set up as a large recreation hall with pool tables, ping-pong tables, card games, and desks with paper and pen to write letters home. They provided servicemen and families with coffee and doughnuts in the morning and sandwiches during the day. The USO also showed movies in the evenings and held dances on Saturday nights.

I hit the jackpot when I met a lady we called Aunt Jimmy. She rented a room to Bill and me for $7 a week, which also included kitchen privileges. Aunt Jimmy was in her early 70s, a widow, and the sweetest lady we ever met. She had long hair twisted into a crown, and I used to wash it for her. We really grew to love each other. When Bill returned home from the base and gave me a hug and kiss, she was always ready and waiting for her hug too. I only ever made a few meals on my own. Aunt Jimmy suggested that we eat together, and she enjoyed cooking for us. I think she was afraid I would make Bill sick with my cooking. Now, we had room and board for only $7 a week. I later got a job so I could at least help out with the groceries.

Aunt Jimmy made the best cake I ever tasted. It was really yellow from all of the eggs she put in the batter. The thought of her home-smoked ham with red gravy still makes my mouth water to this day. In the evenings the three of us used to sit on the porch drinking her homemade lemonade. She loved us like her own children and together we felt like such a loving family. She did not take life too seriously, so my little mistakes made her laugh hysterically. By now, anyone could realize that I had a real affinity for making serious blunders along the way.

One of Aunt Jimmy's other specialties was making the best clabber-milk biscuits I have ever tasted. She used to make them each night with our supper. Clabber was the base ingredient, which is simply milk left out until it turns sour and becomes the consistency of soft cottage cheese. We were eating well, but I would not say that we were eating healthy. I watched in amazement, as Aunt Jimmy never bothered with measuring cups. She would just take a couple handfuls of flour, a scoop of lard, and enough clabber to make it the right consistency. Then she would knead it together and have biscuits ready for baking.

One day I decided I could do the same thing. Under her supervision, I was going to make biscuits. I put that big wooden bowl between my legs, threw in a few handfuls of flour, scooped in some lard and just the right amount of clabber, and began to knead. "Oh my," I though to myself, "How could I possibly knead this gunk together when I was up to my wrists in wallpaper paste?" After awhile I began to give up on my little disaster, but I'll be darned if, after I pulled myself out of this mess, Aunt Jimmy didn't step in and add a little of this and a little of that to successfully save the biscuits. It was amazing. At supper I told Bill that I made half of the biscuits. He was very impressed thinking that I made six and Aunt Jimmy made six. Then I had to tell him "no, I actually made a flopping mess of the first half and Aunt Jimmy repaired the second half."

My first day washing clothes was also an adventure. This was not an area of the country with washers and dryers. People here washed their clothes outside in heated tubs. Once again I thought I could just watch once on my own and learn how to do this without any problem. I started up a good wood fire, and thought, "Wow, that looks good." Next I put the big black iron pot on the fire and left it to get good and hot. When the pot was hot enough, I added the soap and our nice white underwear along with a dark green robe I had given Bill as a wedding gift. Then I stirred the wash to literally cook the clothes until they were clean. When I started to pull the clothes from the water, much to my dismay, I realized I had actually been stirring the water to distribute the color evenly. All of our clothes came out green. Thank heavens I did not put Bill's uniforms in the pot. My dresses were always washed by hand so they were safe. Bill must have done his uniforms at the base, because in boot camp they learned to wash and iron their uniforms so they looked perfect. His uniforms always looked better that anything I ever could have done. When Aunt Jimmy came out and saw the clothesline filled with green clothes, she just about split her sides laughing. By now I guess Bill was getting used to my antics and just accepted these things as normal, or as normal as could be expected.

Many years later, when Bill was in his 60s, a friend asked Bill how he could ever live with me. His reply was, "It's easy, and it's fun. When you get up in the morning, you know pretty well what the day will bring. When I get up in the morning, I haven't the slightest idea what my day will bring, but it's going to be interesting."

Aunt Jimmy also had chickens on her property. One of Bill's chores around the house was to feed the chickens and collect the eggs. Bill found out quickly that he had to go into the chicken coop armed for battle because the rooster from hell protected it. Every time Bill went in that rooster would try and attack with all of his might. Unfortunately, the rooster did not realize he was messing with a Marine. When Bill had enough with the pecking, the rooster ended up with his neck rung, and we ended up with chicken for supper. Fortunately for us, this was okay by Aunt Jimmy because Bill could do no wrong in her eyes.

One morning Aunt Jimmy told me she was going to "swooch." I thought it was a new dance or something. "You watch. I'll show you how to swooch," Aunt Jimmy said. This was how she cleaned the floors. Since all of the floors were linoleum with no rugs, she would get a bucket of water and send the water sailing across the floor. Next she would break out the swoocher. A swoocher was a bunch of tall grass tied together with a cord at the top and was about the thickness of a baseball at the top. She used this to swooch the water around the floor to clean it. It was a lot of fun. I really think every household should have one.

We were having a great time living together as a family, but I decided I needed to find a job so I could buy groceries for the three of us as well as something nice for Aunt Jimmy. I went to the local five-and-dime store in town. Mr. Smith, who ran the store, originally hailed from New York City. He was a nice looking man, approximately 45 years old, and a very pleasant person. His office was upstairs on an open balcony in the back of the store. I walked up the balcony and greeted him with the nicest hello I had in me. He said he would like to help me but really did not need any more employees. On my way to his office I had passed a counter heaped with unmatched pairs of shoes. The wheels started turning in my head. I offered Mr. Smith a deal. I said, "You will never sell those shoes because of the way that counter looks. Let me fix it up for you. If I don't start to sell those shoes in the next two weeks, you can fire me without any pay for those two weeks." We had a deal since he really could not lose. Boy, did I ever work on that counter. Every shoe found its mate, and all the sizes were in order. I felt personally rewarded because I started to sell quite a few pairs of shoes, and most importantly, I had a job. I always felt that somehow, some way, I was going to figure out a way to find places to live and work in every city or town where Bill was transferred. I had long decided that leaving Bill while he was still in this country was not an option.

I only had one small problem working in the store. Along the back wall under the balcony, they sold pickles from enormous jars. They were quite a weakness for me. If Mr. Smith did not see me at any of the counters he would lean over the balcony railing and call out, "Mrs. Moore, get out of the pickle jars." I could not even holler back an excuse to him because my mouth was usually full of pickles. For some reason, he never got mad at me. When I left Kinston, he said that if Bill and I ever came back, there would be a job waiting for me at the store. That was nice of him to say. Unfortunately, we never did get back to Kinston. We only lived there for about five months. It was a sad day when we had to leave Aunt Jimmy. I used to write her so she knew Bill was okay, but she died in 1951, before we could see her again.

To understand why I was such a dingbat and so uneducated about domestic chores like cooking and sorting laundry, I guess I have to explain more about my family history and upbringing. My paternal grandparents came to America before World War I. My grandfather was a high commander in the Kaiser's Army in Germany, and my grandmother came from German aristocracy. She was a beautiful, soft-spoken, and dignified lady. All together, my grandparents had five boys and three girls. Even with all of these children, I was the only female grandchild. My dad, brother, and I visited my grandparents on their estate when I was very young, maybe 3 years old. I asked my brother to describe it to be sure that I was remembering their home correctly. He said he remembered it well. The grounds were like a park. As a matter of fact, the estate later became Passaic Park in New Jersey. Their home was built up on a knoll. It was a huge stone castle with tall turrets on each side. They had a maid who answered the door, and inside there was a big vestibule with rooms off to the sides along with a staircase like the one in "Gone With the Wind." At the top of the staircase was a large stained glass window. Later, this home became the Passaic Public Library.

During World War I, my grandparents lost most of their money that was still invested in Germany. They lost even more in America during the Great Depression. I was still very young when they either lost or had to relinquish their estate and move into a small home in Clifton, New Jersey.

My grandmother decided that I must learn to be a lady, and my mother gladly went along with it since she had big plans for me. Once a week I had to go to their house, and my grandfather would try to teach me to speak German. I was a hopeless cause. My brother also had to go once a week, but he became fluent in the language and could hold a regular conversation in German.

I also had to go once a week for afternoon lessons with my Grandma, also named Mina, where I learned how to conduct myself at high tea, how to correctly hold a teacup, how to sit, and how to position my head. Anyone who knows me now has a great deal of difficulty picturing me sitting like a lady at high tea. In addition, I was taught to walk by balancing a book on my head. My mother was given strict instructions by my grandmother about how I was to be brought up, and it certainly did not include anything domestic. It included piano lessons and handwork, not cooking and cleaning. This is why I had such a hard time handling simple chores around the house. I should have learned these lessons years ago but they were never taught to me. I can only sit back and laugh now, thinking about my grandmother's reaction to the idea that I would later drive a tractor and milk cows.

I never could understand why the Marine Corps moved us so often, especially since our next move was straight back to Beaufort, North Carolina. I sure wish I knew someone in higher places to stop all of this moving, but I am afraid that was not my calling. This time when I packed the suitcase, my only addition was a picture of Aunt Jimmy. I wished, though, that I had remembered to take one of those big jars of pickles for the trip.

As soon as I arrived back in Beaufort, I immediately headed for Rosalie's house. We had only been gone less than a year, but much to my surprise, she had moved into a new house. It was a little bit smaller than her last house. Her husband built it for her as a bribe to keep her from leaving. It did not work. The house was off by itself at the end of

Main Street. There was no reason to even bother asking for a room. It was a small place, and those two had too many problems of their own to have me hanging around.

I left word for Bill at Rosalie's old house because that was where he would come looking for me. Even I could not believe where we ended up living next. I remembered from my first stay in Beaufort that another lady in town named Nettie might have a place to rent. Nettie lived only four houses up from Rosalie's, and luckily she remembered me from my last stay in Beaufort. Much to my surprise, we were not renting a room this time but rather the equivalent of an old U-Haul trailer situated in their backyard. Someone had lived in it before because they had put an old door on the side for an entrance. We were welcome to use the trailer rent-free. We only had to pay a few dollars a week to get water from the outside faucet and to use her bathroom. Of course, there was no electricity. We only had an old mattress and kerosene stove in our trailer. Nettie came up with a kerosene lamp, some pots, a quilt, and some other odds and ends to get us by. It was fortunate for us that both Rosalie and Nettie were very helpful and kind. I guess not much happened in the everyday lives of small town folks, so someone new in the area was cause for big excitement. The town was so small that Bill and I used to get invited to people's porches just so they could meet someone new.

The trailer was only about 10 feet long, but luckily it was high enough to stand in. When Bill first saw it, he thought it was pretty cool to be living in a box, plus he knew the guys on base were going to love this one. I firmly believe we had to be quite compatible to get along with our lifestyle at the time. It could easily make or break our marriage.

Next we noticed that the back wall behind the mattress had hinges. Sure enough, the top half lifted up so we could put a stick under it to prop it up. This was a nice touch because we could now let in sunlight and fresh air. Actually, fresh air might be a stretch because right next to us was a pigpen complete with two pigs. I must say they were considerate pigs as they did not make much noise. Now I had two pets: a little fragrant, but likeable. Later I also found a wild kitten that I worked with but never could calm down enough to pick up. I had my

An American Love Story

pets, and Bill was home every night. Despite the living arrangements, we were enjoying our life together.

When we were settled in our new home, I decided to try my hand at cooking since we had a store where I could shop at everyday. Of course I could not buy anything that needed to be kept cold since it would spoil, living outside with no electricity. I felt like I was on my own this time since I no longer had Aunt Jimmy to bail me out when I got into trouble, but at least the store in town had plenty of different foods for me to experiment with each day. I wrote a letter to my mother-in-law and asked her to send me one of her many cookbooks. In a little over a week's time, I received a paperback cookbook from Moms. Armed with my cookbook, I was determined to start making edible meals on my little two-burner kerosene stove. I was proud of myself because we now ate pasta with homemade sauce, stew, pot roast, pork and sauerkraut, and fried eggs sunny-side up. Cooking was also a challenge because we had no oven, so everything was cooked on the stovetop. Bill was very impressed with my progress as a cook. He fixed up a ring outside and put a grate on it so we could even cook on an open grill. I was now feeling like Chef Pierre.

Since we were cooking at home each evening, we had to come up with a way to wash our dishes. Nettie was kind enough to provide us with a small metal dishpan. First we had to go back to the side of the house and get more water to wash the dishes. Next we heated the water on the kerosene stove. When the water was warm enough, we moved it on top of a large box that contained our utensils and dishes. I washed and Bill dried while he sat on the bed because we did not have enough room for both of us to stand next to each other. I would wash a dish and turn around and hand it to him on the bed. We did not have a rinse cycle for the dishes but we figured a little soap would never hurt us.

Laundry was another adventure. It was done outside in a washtub with a scrub board. Someone needs to go back in time, find the person that invented the scrub board, and shoot them without remorse. My hands were always raw and bleeding from this contraption. However, I quickly learned that if I washed the whites before the colored clothes, I could use the same water for both loads. I needed multiple tubs of water to rinse out the laundry. When I finished washing the clothes, I hung them on the line outside to dry. There was nothing to it, except we still had a line full of green clothes from my first wash mishap in Kinston. Luckily Bill was Irish so I think he liked to see me in green underwear and nightgowns.

I don't remember why, but one evening Nettie invited us to spend the night inside with her. After dinner, we sat in the living room circled around a roaring fire in an old potbelly stove. For most of the evening I could not even look Bill in the face because I was afraid I would crack up and embarrass us all. Nettie sat in a rocker about a leg's length away from the stove. Every so often her leg would rise and she would kick the door open on the stove with her foot. Without skipping a beat, she would spit her tobacco juice into the fire and then close the door. She would never miss. I challenge anyone to spend an evening watching that kind of talent and not falling on the floor laughing.

When the evening wound down, Nettie showed us to our bedroom and our jaws almost dropped to the floor. Standing before us was a real backcountry featherbed that she had spent years stuffing with chicken feathers. We had never seen a bed that was so high in our lives. When we climbed in, we started to sink in so deeply that I could barely see Bill, who was only a few feet away from me. It was like sleeping on a cloud. Today's waterbeds have nothing on an old fashioned featherbed.

Bill brought home some chewing tobacco from the base to thank Nettie for our evening. That was probably the best gift we could have given her. We enjoyed quite a few months in the backyard. I would get to visit with Rosalie from time to time, and I also made a few other friends in town. Beaufort was actually starting to feel like home for us, which could only mean one thing – it was time for the Marine Corps to move us someplace else.

This time we had the opportunity to leave North Carolina for Arkansas in September, 1944. Bill also received the good news that he was being promoted to staff sergeant. For this move, I only added a cookbook to my belongings. In order to get to the base in Arkansas, I first had to take a five-hour bus ride from Beaufort to Rocky Mountain, North Carolina. From there I boarded a train headed for Arkansas. I am not talking about Amtrak, I mean an old coal-fired, cinder-throwing locomotive that did everything but start chanting, "I think I can, I think I can." The cars had straight-back seats, no dining car, and no stops for getting out and stretching your legs. The train only stopped briefly to pick up and drop off passengers. At one of the stops, I saw a lady outside selling egg sandwiches and orange soda. Neither one of these particularly appealed to me, but I was quite hungry and thirsty and there were no other options in sight. I quickly ate my sandwich and drank my soda, and shortly thereafter I became so violently ill that I spent the rest of the trip – from that afternoon until the next day when we arrived – curled up in the aisle in the back of the car.

Although I felt so bad, I was thinking it was no fun for Bill either because he was in a jeep convoy traveling all the way from North Carolina to Arkansas. As it turned out, however, they were welcomed with open arms in every town, put up in hotels with tons of food, and even enjoyed entertainment one night. The sergeant thought they were possibly mistaken for combat Marines, but he decided not to correct the townspeople and let his troops enjoy the hospitality. I guess I should have only felt sorry for myself on the train since Bill was in such good hands.

Finally, I arrived in Little Rock, Arkansas. I was to meet up with Bill at the local USO. Normally, wherever I arrived, the servicemen were polite and helpful and always offered to carry my suitcase. Not this time. I was a disheveled mess and must have reeked from the long train ride and remnants of the egg sandwich, so everyone stayed clear of me. I lugged my suitcase to the nearest hotel and plopped down for the night. In the morning I headed for the USO, had a coffee and doughnut there, and to my dismay found out that Little Rock actually had four USOs in the city. This messed up our usual plan for meeting in a set place.

I knew Bill's new base was located in Newport, Arkansas, about an hour northeast of Little Rock. I decided that instead of walking around the hot city of Little Rock to visit each USO, I would just take the local train to Newport and find Bill near the base. So now, the key was to find Bill before he headed to Little Rock to try and find me. Bill's convoy was scheduled to take five days to travel from North Carolina to Arkansas, so I had at least two days to wait for him. I found a room at a place called the Hotel Lavoy for $3 a night and headed out to the local USO.

Newport had a population of 1,000 people at most, and I think most of them were direct descendents of the first generation in the area. The town was a decent size for the area with a food store, liquor store, bakery, and general store, along with a shoemaker, a doctor, and a dentist. They were all mom-and-pop businesses that made their money on Saturdays when everyone came down from the hills.

My master plan was to stay all day at the USO and ask every Marine I saw to please find Bill Moore when the jeep convoy arrived from North Carolina and let him know his wife was at the Hotel Lavoy in town, not in Little Rock. Lord knows how many Marines I spoke to and thought were out looking for my husband. It turns out that on the following evening, Bill had liberty and headed to see me at the Hotel Lavoy. When I opened the hotel room door, much to my surprise I was not greeted with hugs and kisses. All Bill said to me was, "Do you have any idea what it is like to have half of the Marine Corps tell me that my wife is at the Hotel Lavoy?" Apparently, some of the Marines decided to add a little extra to the message. I told him that I thought it was a pretty good idea at the time. He just shook his head and then I finally got my hug and kiss.

We went out to dinner at a cheap little Mexican restaurant with really good food. Bill told me the goods news that along with his promotion he was assigned to one of the housing units on base. Bill was as thrilled as I was to live right on base and not have to hunt down a place to live for once. He did, however, have one request. He asked me, "Honey, with you living on base, can you try hard to be a good little wife and not get me thrown into the brig?" I thought they could not possibly do that because of my antics, but this is the military and they were in charge. I just always believed that someone was watching over me with an even higher authority than the military.

We scraped by with very little money, but it was a much different time in the 1940s. Prices were so much less than they are today. Most people who grew up in later generations could not believe what we paid for staple items. A loaf of bread cost a nickel, ground meat was 25 cents per pound, and we could eat dinner out for $1.25. The hotels I stayed in were around $3 a night. If we really got in a bind, we could always go to the Red Cross for help. I had to do this one time after I used the last of my money on train fare. I borrowed $20 to pay the rent. They only asked to give back what you could afford, if possible. I paid it all back in a couple of months.

I moved on to the base with Bill. The residences were more like a row of barracks divided into apartments. We lived among 40 enlisted families who were lucky enough to qualify for housing. Many of the bases where Bill was previously stationed were so small that they only contained housing for the officers and their families. Each apartment contained a fairly good-sized room that served as a kitchen and front room. It also had a bedroom and a bathroom. What a luxury it was to be able to shower whenever we wanted, especially compared to Nettie's where we were allowed to shower just once a week, on Saturday nights. Our kitchen had a kerosene stove with a sink and icebox. Our front room had a table and two folding chairs. Bill was in charge of the furnishings on base so we wound up with one of the few double beds. This made us the envy of our friends. He also snuck in a twin bed that we used for a couch in the front room. Bill brought in some extra sheets which I dyed yellow and used for curtains, a bedspread, and a tablecloth. It looked friendly when I was finished. Far and away, it was the nicest place we had lived to date.

Since I had been on my own for a short time and had become more comfortable cooking, I decided to invite our friends over for dinner. I felt this was pretty brave of me considering the circumstances. I made pot roast with mashed potatoes, string beans, and a salad, along with pineapple upside down cake for desert. I wore a little cotton dress with a fancy apron, and I felt like such a wife and homemaker for the evening. Our guests ate everything and thanked me. I hoped they were not just being polite.

We ate very well in Arkansas, especially since most of the food was home grown. Because meat prices were based on the kind of meat such as beef, pork, or veal, and not according to the cut, we ate a lot of steak and prime rib. The best part was that the chickens were already killed and defeathered.

I applied for a job on base and was hired to work in the PX (Military for Postal Exchange). Here we sold everything from toiletries, moccasins, underwear, and over-the-counter drugs to jewelry and gift items. Three of the wives worked in the PX. I am not sure if anyone today is familiar with blitz cloth, but it made anything shine. I was working the jewelry counter one afternoon when I decided the copper fish pins needed a good cleaning. I decided I could really shine them up with the blitz cloth. I cleaned them up all right. I took all of the copper right off them. The only way I could cover up my mistake was to do the same thing to all of the fish pins. Luckily it worked. All of the pins sold and no one knew the difference.

Every morning the prisoners on the base scrubbed the PX floor. They were mostly the fellows being disciplined for minor offenses. We took turns opening the PX in the morning. On one of my mornings, the prisoners were scrubbing away when I turned on the juke box, and we all started doing the jitterbug. We were having a good time until the sergeant walked in. Luckily, he did not give us too hard of a time. He just told everyone to get back to work. He gave me a look but did not report us. There was both a sergeant and lieutenant in charge of the PX, but they never stayed long. They would primarily check in on things, do a little paperwork, and leave. There were days when all personnel were required to attend some type of event on base. These were boring days with very few customers which inevitably lead me to cause problems for myself, like cleaning the copper off of the fish pins.

One day our lieutenant left for the day to attend a meeting in Cherry Hill, North Carolina, and left the sergeant in charge. There were no customers around, so all of us decided to shut down the PX. Unbeknownst to us, the lieutenant's flight was cancelled, so he came back to close up the PX only to find it deserted. In the morning he was waiting for us. All of us swore that the sergeant knew nothing of what we did and that we made the decision on our own after the sergeant had left. From that day on, the sergeant was always very nice to us for taking the blame for him. We could have ended up getting fired and the sergeant could have been demoted, but luckily it blew over.

Every weekend on the outskirts of town some people set up a tent where a brute of a man challenged anyone in the crowd to fight him for prize money. The prize money came from the others that fought this huge man first. We only went to the fights once. It was brutal. By the end of the evening, the tent was a free-for-all so we got out as fast as possible. Our main entertainment on the weekends was waiting for the Okies to come down from the hills and lose all of their money to a bunch of con artists who set up shell games and other games of chance outside of the tent. I am sure most of those people lost all of their money each Saturday, but surely enough they would come back again the following weekend just to lose more.

We were still stationed in Arkansas in December of 1944, and we were starting to think about our second Christmas together as husband and wife. Unfortunately, the Marine Corps was also thinking about Christmas, but in a much different way. On December 25, 1944, Bill's unit was to be shipped overseas. Bill came home to break the news to me by plopping a bottle of whiskey on the table and saying, "I think we are going to need this tonight." Soon after he told me the news, neither of us wanted to drink. We instead wanted to clearly remember every moment of our last night together. So, we poured the whiskey down the sink and never took a sip.

The next day all of the wives stood alongside the road as we watched our husbands march off in full combat gear to the end of the base where a convoy of trucks was waiting to pick them up. Our husbands, the fellows we befriended at the PX, the friends whose problems we listened to and joys we shared, the gentlemen we congratulated for becoming a new Daddy or comforted when they received a "Dear John" letter, marched down the road. As I watched them fade into the distance, all of the life drained out of me. "Merry Christmas," I thought to myself.

From that moment until they reached the islands in the Pacific, I was completely in the dark as to what Bill was doing. They were not allowed to write or call while they were still in the United States waiting to be shipped overseas. For the most part, they could not tell us anything because they did not know either. Everything was kept a secret until the last possible moment during the war.

The next day I packed up my suitcase for the last time and headed home to my parents house in New Jersey. Naturally I was devastated from the previous day, but I had no regrets about choosing to follow Bill for as long as possible. We had two eventful years together before he was shipped overseas, and I had a ton of memories to think about while we were separated.

It took a full month before I received my first letter from Bill. The mail was censored by the military so most of us made up some sort of code with our husbands so we could get a general idea of where they were stationed. For the most part, it worked pretty well. We sectioned off a map of the Pacific Ocean with different letters. The code was fairly simple, he would close each letter with a sentence like, "P.S.: Did Mary have her baby yet?" Since we did not know a Mary that was pregnant, I would look under the section we had marked "M." On our map, this stood for the Marshall Islands. We had to keep the sentences fairly benign and generic or the military censors would black the line out before it was sent. Later on I received a letter with a strange P.S. at the end. It took some searching but I deduced he was on the small island of Enewetak. I had Bill pinpointed pretty close to where he was stationed, and I knew there was no action going on at the time. This was a big comfort to me.

I lived with my parents while Bill was overseas so I could save as much money as possible. Bill also sent home the money that he won playing pinochle. All of it went into our savings account. My parents had a fairly nice home in Ridgewood. It was a quaint, upscale, neighborhood. Many of our neighbors worked in New York City as bankers on Wall Street. Owners of large companies also lived in the town including the founder of Birdseye Frozen Foods. I guess this is why my mother finally consented to buying the house after renting for all of those years. It was a status symbol to live in the neighborhood. The home was furnished in all dark mahogany, with a beautiful piano, brocaded upholstery, oriental rugs, and leaded crystal everywhere. I remember flicking the crystal with my finger and hearing it ring a beautiful note for a long time. There were three bedrooms and a bath upstairs in addition to the ones downstairs. My father had a large vegetable garden and grew everything imaginable. When he canned the vegetables, it fed us for the year. This was extremely helpful at the time because most families were expected to grow victory gardens to supplement the food rations.

I wrote Bill every day, and he wrote me about three times a week. At the time a regular letter cost 3 cents to mail, but Victory Mail, which was a small page with about a 4-inch by 3-inch space to write in, was free. I would address the letters to the APO, or Army Post Office, with Bill's complete name and squadron number. The letter was then forwarded by the armed services to the correct location and usually took about two weeks to deliver in either direction. He would tell me about the beautiful sunsets out on the Pacific and how he wished I could be there to share them with him. The island, called Enewetak, was just two miles long and a quarter-mile wide. It only had a few palm trees and some dogs running around. The natives from the other islands would canoe over after dark to collect some of the dogs for dinner. After the war, this was one of the many islands where nuclear bombs were tested. It was not suitable again for habitation until the 1980's.

The Marines did not have much to do on the island except run some drills each day, and then they relaxed by playing baseball or cards. Sometimes they swam in the ocean, read, or wrote letters home. Bill spent almost a year on this tiny island, as did many other units on the surrounding islands, waiting for the order to invade Japan. Everyone knew the invasion would have been massive, similar to D-Day in Europe, and the casualties would have been just as bad, if not worse.

Back at home I worked 10- to 14-hour shifts a day as a waitress in the Tree Tavern in Patterson, New Jersey. My mother-in-law worked there and told me it was a great place for tips. The Tree Tavern was known for its excellent Italian food. Restaurants did not have to ration food like the general public, so people would eat out if they could afford it in order to stretch out their meat stamps. The restaurant was always filled to capacity so I could count on at least $50 in tips each night and even more on weekends.

I spent some of the money for room and board at home or for packages I sent to Bill, but I put most of it in the bank for our future. I also spent my time making things for our hope chest. It was quite full with a small set of dishes, towels, bed sheets, and silverware. I also added some cookware I earned from saving General Mills coupons. In addition, I placed in some pictures I embroidered, doilies I crocheted, and a blue blanket – all of it waiting for Bill's return. I would often go into our hope chest, take everything out, look at it, and dream of Bill coming home soon. I could not wait to have a place of our own to use these things. How I prayed this would happen soon.

Chapter 5
MY BROTHER BILL

My brother, Bill Haessner, who I am so proud of, enlisted in the Army Air Corps in the spring of 1942 and was sent overseas immediately without any training. He was sent to Australia and served in the 33rd Squadron, 374 Group, 5th wing, 5th Air Force Squadron, stationed in Brisbane, Australia. My brother did not come home again until June of 1945. Bill was assigned as a flight engineer on a troop carrier. His duty was to maintain the plane while the squadron evacuated the wounded or dropped off paratroopers, medical supplies, food supplies, and ammunition to combat areas. These flights were lifelines for the troops. They worked in tandem with Australian units who my brother greatly admired and respected for their bravery. In many of the areas where they were stationed, such as Port Moresby in current day Papua New Guinea, the Japanese were everywhere from the edge of the landing strip to less than 10 miles out in the jungle, constantly shooting at the planes as they passed by.

Bill flew over or near enemy lines to provide supplies to the U.S. troops who were battling to cut off the supply lines of the Japanese soldiers. When the supply lines for food, medical supplies, or ammunition were cut off, the soldiers were basically forgotten about by both the Americans and the Japanese and left in the jungle to die. This is how the Americans were forced to fight from island to island in the Pacific. When the areas near Australia and New Zealand were completed, they headed to the next airstrip and continued in the same manner all the way across New Guinea until they reached the Philippines. These airstrips were not the usual landing strips. They were coral reefs and paths of cut grass in the jungle, or many times they were short strips on the side of a mountain. The planes would take off downhill to gain as much speed as possible and land uphill to adjust for the short landing area. Many of Bill's buddies were lost on these landings. As a matter of fact, before a crew headed out on a run, they would designate who would get their boots if they did not make it back because boots were in such big demand. Soldiers' boots quickly rotted in the jungle heat and would not last at all unless they cut the toes out and ripped slits in the sides for air circulation.

The squadron consisted of 12 planes total. Each plane crew consisted of four soldiers on board and two on the ground. Some days they would run eight missions in a 24-hour period. I asked my brother how he felt risking his life day in and day out. His answer was, "We had a job to do and the combat soldiers were depending on us." Dying was not something he or his fellow soldiers thought about. It was more of an accepted fact that they would most likely not return home alive. Their thoughts were not on whether they would make it home, but rather who would die next. Someone living back in the United States could never truly understand what Bill and his fellow soldiers were going through. They were shot at by snipers in the jungle as they got into their planes, they were shot at during take-off, they were shot at when they flew close to the front lines, and they were shot at again when returning from their mission.

As one could imagine, Bill's squadron became extremely close knit. It bothered all of them immensely when one of their fellow soldiers was killed, especially since there was a good chance that the soldier had saved one of their lives on a number of occasions. To this day, at 86, my brother still chokes up just thinking about the men he served with who lost their lives during the war.

Bill flew out of an area near Port Moresby in Papau, New Guinea. There were no roads in this area of New Guinea, just paths cut out of the jungle to link one tribal village to another. The people living in New Guinea were not part of the war until the Japanese invaded the island in 1942 to set up a base camp for a planned invasion of Australia. The island became famous for the bravery of a group of people nicknamed the Fuzzy Wuzzy Angels who rescued injured soldiers and carried them back to medical facilities. Their heroic acts during the war have been written about in poems and are part of Australian folklore. The Fuzzy Wuzzy Angels learned to speak English from the missionaries who lived on the island before the war. They were more or less the law enforcement on the island and the only natives who carried guns.

The responsibility for the flights, in addition to the physical and mental exhaustion of the situation, took a toll on my brother and affected him for the rest of his life. Bill was sent back to the United States in June of 1945 where he finished out his service by flying wounded soldiers out at sea back to hospitals in the area or flying from small islands back to the mainland. This job was much easier on him. For the first time in three years, Bill was able to sleep in a real bed and eat regular food instead of k-rations. When the war ended, Bill was sent to a Veterans Affairs (VA) hospital in New Jersey for treatment. Instead of helping him, the doctors drugged him and never attempted to treat his symptoms. Today he would have been diagnosed with post-traumatic stress disorder, but in the 1940s doctors had little clue how to treat soldiers coming home from the war. Instead of remaining on the medications, Bill walked out of the hospital, hopped on a bus, and headed back to our home in Passaic.

At home he saw our family doctor, and Bill begged him not to put him on any kind of medication. The doctor told him he would not prescribe any pills but advised Bill to drink a shot of whiskey to help with his nerves. Bill could not handle hard alcohol so he drank beer instead. Bill would wait for me to get home from work, and we would go to a small bar together. We would have a drink and dance together slowly until the owner kicked us out. He needed to be held and to be close to someone. When he first returned home, he could not even speak; he could only express himself through grunts and tears. Slowly he started to relax a little and could manage to speak a word or two.

It took about three months before he started to talk. He could barely hold a conversation, but he managed on his own. He suffered from seizures brought on by the stress of the war. Although they began to occur less often, it still took many years for them to stop altogether.

Bill could not handle the atmosphere in our home, so he bought a horse and a dog and moved to a dude ranch near Peekskill, New York, called Cimarron Ranch. He was a working guest. There he met a girl name Jodie who he married but later divorced. Bill was biding his time until his old friend Hans was out of the Navy. Hans was a pilot in the Navy and, together with Bill's engineering training from the Marines; they planned on starting a transport service in Alaska.

Tragically, this dream never came true. At a time when my brother did not need any more hardship, he was dealt another critical blow to his health. Hans was flying some officers over the state of New York when the plane he was flying crashed a short distance from the dude ranch where my brother was staying. Bill was with the search party that found the plane. No one survived the crash. I cannot even imagine the devastation my brother felt, especially during a time of his life when he was so fragile.

I developed a large soft spot in my heart for my brother after everything he went through in the war. My husband shared the same feelings. My brother witnessed some horrific events during World War II, most of which he never spoke of to anyone, not even me. The memories haunted him throughout the rest of his life, and it really took a toll on him.

My brother left the Army with an honorable discharge. He was qualified to wear the Air Medal, the Good Conduct Medal, the Asiatic-Pacific Campaign Medal, and the Presidential Unit Citation with an oak leaf cluster. He also received a letter from Lieutenant General George C. Kenney for meritorious achievement. That letter was sent to my parents, and I have it today.

Chapter 6
PEACE DECLARED

As my brother was coming home and trying to recover from the war, little did I know my husband was somewhere on an island in the Pacific Ocean training with his fellow Marines for the imminent invasion of Japan. One of the letters I received from Bill kept asking, "What is wrong? When I read your letters lately I feel something is wrong. What is it?" It was such a torturous feeling to know that Bill had no idea what I was going through back home trying to help my brother. Bill was so many miles away, and I can only imagine the many different thoughts that entered his mind. I wished there was some way I could get in touch with him quickly, but of course there was no way to reach him by phone. All we had were the letters we wrote back and forth. When Bill asked me a question in a letter, not only did he have to wait the two weeks it took the letter to reach me in New Jersey, but then he would have to wait another two weeks to receive my response.

I tried to explain to Bill that the stress he felt in the letters was coming from the strain I was putting on myself to help my brother. Many times I stayed up with Bill into the early morning hours after working a full shift at the restaurant. Between work, my brother, and trying to write letters each day, I just did not have much time for sleep. This was underscored by the fact that my husband was somewhere on an island in the Pacific Ocean and I had no idea if or when I would ever see him again. With all of this on my mind, the letters I wrote must have started to reveal some of the strain I was feeling. Not long after I received Bill's letter, I collapsed at work from exhaustion. The only option was for me to quit my job. Bill was relieved, and he understood that it was much more important for me to take care of my brother. So I headed up to the ranch to be with my brother for two weeks.

In early May of 1945, when the war ended in Europe, it was a relief but not yet cause for a full celebration. May 8, 1945, is known in the history books as V-E Day, but many of the people I knew around me in New Jersey only felt like it was the first step. For us, the war had to also end in the Pacific before the true celebration could begin. Many families around us had sons in both Europe and Asia. It was hard to celebrate for one half of a family when the other half was still at war. In addition, people had no idea how long the war in the Pacific was going to last. That is the reason why Marines like my husband were preparing for an invasion of Japan – to end the war once and for all.

Not long after I returned home from visiting my brother at Cimarron Ranch, the first atomic bomb was dropped on the city of Hiroshima, Japan, on August 6, 1945, at 8:15 a.m. When the news broke, fire and police sirens as well as factory whistles blew all over town. People realized this meant that the war would end very soon. Three days later, the second and final atomic weapon ever used in war was dropped on the city of Nagasaki. I pray for all of those poor people who were killed or injured by the bomb. I know many innocent people died from these attacks. But it was through this action that my Bill, along with literally hundreds of thousands of soldiers in all branches of the military, would no longer be needed to invade Japan. Who knows how many young men were now able to come home and start families instead of dying in a final invasion. On August 14, 1945, Japan surrendered and the war was finally over. I will never ever forget that day. People were running up and down the streets and sidewalks yelling with joy. I drove all around town honking my horn constantly, along with friends and strangers in the neighborhood. When I walked around town, I stopped anyone – I did not care who they were – and I hugged and kissed them saying, "My Bill is coming home." In the year 2005 as I write this, the tears are rolling down my cheeks as I remember that wonderful, wonderful, emotional day. It was noisier and more boisterous than any New Year's Eve celebration I ever attended.

About two weeks after peace was declared, I received a letter from Bill that said, "I'm coming home, honey." In my mind, I thought this meant I would see him some time in September, but that is not quite how the Marines operated. The armed forces had literally hundreds of thousands of troops to bring back to the United States, so it took quite awhile to get back home. Each group had to wait their turn for a ship. Not only did Bill have to stay on the small island of Enewetak for another 60 days after the war ended, but the troop ship carrying him home took a month to sail across the Pacific to reach California. (Of course it did have a stop in Hawaii so it must not have been too bad.)

At one point I wrote to Bill and told him I wanted to travel to California to meet him in San Diego when he arrived. He appreciated the sentiment but told me he had no way of knowing when he would reach the West Coast, so it was not possible to make the arrangements. I had no choice but to stay at home in New Jersey and wait impatiently for my husband to arrive back in the United States for the first time in a year. I was so anxious that I could not even comprehend what other wives or fiancées who may not have seen their loved ones in two or three years were going through.

Bill finally arrived in San Diego in early December, and he called me as soon as he could find a phone. He had to stay in California for about two weeks, but he called me collect every night, so by the end of his stay I owed my parents a bundle for the phone bill. Bill's only trip to the West Coast was when he shipped out to war, so he spent some of his time roaming around San Diego. He even had an opportunity to spend a day at the San Diego Zoo, and he was very impressed by the way the animals were kept in natural habitats instead of cages like the zoos he had visited back East. He knew how I liked animals, so he vowed that some day we would get back to the San Diego Zoo together.

When Bill was finally allowed to leave San Diego in late December, he hopped aboard a train headed for the East Coast. It took six days to reach New Jersey. He rode on an old steam train that did not have a place to shower, shave, or even change clothes during the trip. The train arrived at Union Station in New York City. Bill did not want me to drive into the city alone in his old car, so he hopped on a bus and we met at the George Washington Bridge in Fort Lee, New Jersey.

I was waiting for him with his old green Ford convertible that my father let me keep in the garage while Bill was away. I dressed in my finest and primped my hair because I wanted to look my very best. It seemed to take forever for the bus to arrive from New York, but finally it came into sight. When he stepped off we hugged and kissed while the people standing around clapped and cheered. We saw so many happy homecomings like this every day. Once in the car we just looked at each other and cried. We were finally together, and for us, the war was over. Ironically, Bill arrived home on Christmas Day, exactly one year after I had tearfully said goodbye to him in Arkansas.

Bill and I headed to my parents home for a Christmas celebration. This was our third Christmas as a married couple but our first one together in New Jersey. Bill's mom joined us at my parents home. When it was time to leave, we took Moms to her daughter's house. She was nice enough to offer us her apartment in Patterson, New Jersey, for 10 days until Bill had to leave again. She had a walk-up apartment (meaning no elevator) on the fifth floor. In this type of building, the higher the floor someone lived on, the less rent they were charged. The apartment had two windows in front and two in back with partitions to separate rooms. The apartments did not have central heating so the tenants used kerosene heaters to keep the rooms warm. The kerosene was kept in drums in the cellar so we had to walk downstairs to refill the heater every time it ran out of fuel. I have no idea how someone did not accidentally burn down the building trying to stay warm in the winter.

I could go into more detail, but I really see no reason why I should talk about the next 10 days. It was our honeymoon and I should not have to elaborate on that.

When Bill's leave was up, he had to once again head back to Beaufort, North Carolina, and wait to be mustered out of the Marines. I packed my suitcase once again, complete with my cookbook, and we boarded a train for the trip back to Beaufort. I made some turkey and cranberry sauce sandwiches to eat on the train, which really hit the spot, but the best part of the trip back to North Carolina was cuddling up with my husband secure in the knowledge that he had returned safely from the war.

When we arrived, Bill and I dropped off our suitcases at the Beaufort post office window inside the general store and took a walk along the shoreline. It was a beautiful ocean view but the beach was filled with broken shards of clamshells from the fishery that had dumped them on the beach for many years. We had been gone for just over two years but everything still looked the same in this sleepy little town. The homes were in need of a coat of paint from the harsh salt air and many needed new porches or steps, but most of the residents did not have the money to spend on luxuries such as upkeep on a home.

When we returned to the general store, we spoke to Mr. Lewis, the postmaster. We explained to him that we were looking for a place to live until Bill was discharged from the Marines. Luckily, Mr. Lewis had an old empty house on the corner of Turkey Lane where we could stay for just the cost of electricity and water. After we settled in, it was time for Bill to catch a bus to the base at Cherry Point. At least he knew where to find me when he was out on liberty.

From our last trip to Beaufort, I knew that Turkey Lane was the area of town where all the poor people lived, both black and white alike. Now they could add Bill and me to their social register. To say this was an old house was being very kind. I doubt if it was ever painted again, inside or out, after it was built. We had to walk very carefully on the steps and the porch or otherwise our feet could fall right through the rotted boards.

The interior of the house was just as appealing as the exterior. Entering the front room, we had a potbelly coal stove, two straight chairs, and a small table. The bedroom was on the left off of the front room with a bed, a mattress of sorts, and an old quilt. Someone had hammered long nails into the walls years ago for hanging clothes. Behind the front room was the kitchen and bathroom. There was a back door off of the kitchen but there were no steps, so if I walked out the back I had to jump a good four feet to get to the ground. There was a sink in the kitchen but it did not have running water so we had to use the bathroom sink for our water. We did not have hot water in the bathroom so we heated water in the kitchen on our little kerosene stove to fill the bathtub; it always ended up being a very cool, shallow bath. At least the toilet was in working order, thank goodness, but the bathroom was so tiny that we could wash our hands while sitting on the throne.

By January it was starting to get quite cold and we needed some heat in the house. We purchased a half ton of coal that was dumped on the ground in back of the house. When Bill got home, he figured our coal would most likely be gone by morning if we left it outside. We decided our only option was to use the kitchen as a storage shed. Bill borrowed a shovel from Mr. Lewis, who happened to live three houses down on Main Street, and we shoveled the coal into the kitchen. After that we lost the use of our kitchen, so we put the kerosene cook stove in the front room. The windows actually had glass in them so we were able to stay comfortably warm. After supper we played cards for awhile, and then we were off to bed. Bill's bus left for the base at 5 a.m., and if he missed it he would be in big trouble.

In February, a real cold spell hit. I did not know how people managed because all of the water pipes were above ground. I guess the locals knew the way to save their pipes was to let the water run slowly all night to prevent the pipes from freezing. We were not privy to this information. When I got up in the morning to go to the bathroom, I walked into a winter wonderland. The pipes broke in the bathroom, and as the water sprayed it literally froze. It really was pretty, like an ice cavern with icicles hanging from the ceiling, the sink, and literally everywhere. I called Bill to come in and look at our beautiful bathroom. I must confess he was not as impressed as I was. Luckily everyone in town cooperated with each other. Those whose lines did not crack let others use their toilets and water. With the pipes above ground, it was no time at all before everything was back to normal.

Soon after that, one of Bill's buddies was discharged. He lived in a small apartment, which was really just a bedroom and kitchen that extended out of the back of someone's home. We moved in, and it was more comfortable for the remainder of our short stay in North Carolina. I always wondered how long the coal lasted that we left on the kitchen floor in Mr. Lewis's place.

Finally our dream came true and Bill was discharged from the Marine Corps on March 22, 1946. We could now move back to New

Jersey and think about starting a family. I guess we thought really long and hard about it because nine months later our first daughter, Mina, was born.

My personal thoughts:

I would like to interject a thought at this point. I mentioned putting on my finest clothes for Bill's homecoming in 1945, but now at the age of 81, I live mostly in jeans, dress slacks, or sweats around the house. It was very nice during the 1930's and early '40s when everyone dressed up to go to town, the movies, church, or school. Men and women alike wore nice clothes and fancy hats; it really made us feel good about ourselves. The men enjoyed it just as much as the women. Trips to the beach were not even exempt from dressing for the occasion. Although dresses, fancy hats, and nice shoes were never suitable for a day out at the beach, for some reason it was still the norm. Our heels would sink into the sand, and our hats were always blowing off and floating around the beach. Not to mention, just try and sit on a blanket in the sand with a fancy dress on. At least I wasn't from an era when bathing suits were down to my ankles. Compared to my parents, we were much more modern. Our suits were one-piece outfits that ended about 6 inches above the knee and began with a neckline that actually touched my neck. People who were daring enough to wear a yellow suit instead of the usual navy or black were considered to be quite risqué. What the men were aiming for I have no idea. Their suits were always black with a little length in the legs, but for some reason their suits had large 6 inch by 4 inch ovals cut out of the sides. I never understood what they were trying to show off. It certainly was not their six-pack abs under their armpits. This was all before I became a teenager. By the time I was 14, we started to show a little skin, but not too much. Men in their 70s and 80s must go half out of their minds when they go to the beach nowadays. I am sure that when my brother saw women on the beach in the 1990s he must have been thinking, "Hallelujah! This is what we fought for! Amen."

Chapter 7
OUR HOME AND FAMILY

While we were in Beaufort waiting for Bill's discharge, my parents were very busy at home. Much to our regret, they remodeled the upstairs bedrooms into an apartment for Bill and me. It included a very large bedroom along with a front room about the same size. The bedroom opened up onto a railed deck through French doors. Our apartment also had a kitchen with an electric stove and oven. The oven was something new for me to tackle. Since Bill loved apple pies, I quickly made them my first project. In the back of my mind I knew this apartment was my mother's doing just to keep me near her to make her happy.

Bill got back his job at the garage as a mechanic. On December 3, 1946, our daughter Mina was born. Our Christmas was very special with our new baby girl, however living in my parents home prevented us from truly having our own life. Bill did not let on, but he kept his eyes and ears open for a new place for us to live. In early spring he came home from work really happy. He found us a small house in Ridgewood. It took most of our savings to come up with the $500 down payment, but we gladly took the chance. The house itself was fairly small and in total cost $7,000. Our mortgage payment was $50 a month. Bill was making about $40 a week at the garage, so we knew it would be tight financially, but we could manage. The front room measured about 10 feet by 12 feet and the dining area was 8 feet by 8 feet. The kitchen had just barely enough room to work in and our bedroom and bathrooms were not large either, but it had a tiny room that could hold a crib and dresser for Mina. Bill and my dad spent the weekends painting the inside, and in April of 1947, we moved into our first home together. It may not have been much of a house, but it was ours, and we were happy.

Bill answered an ad in the paper for a mason looking for a laborer. It seemed like a good opportunity for work in the area. After he worked there for a while, his boss told him that as long as he kept the other men supplied with cement and blocks, he could also try his hand at laying brick. Through hard work, he not only learned masonry but he eventually learned all the steps for building an entire house. He put his knowledge to work quickly and built a porch on the front of our house.

Mina just loved to help her dad. As soon as she could walk well enough, she never left his side. If he raked leaves, she raked leaves. If he worked on our car, she was right under it with him. They were pals. During the summer, Bill took Mina to the lake at the Ridgewood Country Park where she learned to swim when she was just a year and a half old. They would swim side-by-side out to a raft; Bill would lift her onto it and she would jump right off, swim under water, and surface up next to him. My heart was always in my throat as I watched even though I was sure Bill certainly knew what he was doing.

In August of 1948 I became pregnant for the second time. I never felt well during my pregnancy. I was always very tired and extremely nervous, and I simply could not understand the reason for it. Our life was in a great place: I was happy to be a mother again, Bill liked his job, and we had a little home of our own. I started to battle a serious bout of anxiety whenever I walked the six blocks into town. I would feel so nervous and anxious that I found myself practically running with the baby carriage, trying to rush back home.

On May 10, 1949, our second daughter, Sandra, was born. We now had two happy and healthy girls, but we had reached an overcrowding point in our small little house in Ridgewood. At the same time, Bill was itching to put his knowledge as a contractor to use for his own family. We decided to look for a piece of land. We found an acre of land for $1,000 near the New York state line in a small town consisting of 1200 people called Ramsey, New Jersey.

Bill's service in the Marines automatically qualified us for a GI loan at 5 percent interest, so we borrowed $5,000 and Bill tackled the job of building our house. My dad helped him when he needed someone to hold the other end of a long board. Every day after he finished his job in Westwood, he drove 15 miles out to the house and worked as long as he could. He would then turn around and drive 20 miles back to our house. Bill decided to frame the house with cement block. He was able to complete the outside before winter set in, which gave him the chance to work on the inside during the cold weather months. I intended to help him on the weekends but my health was getting worse, and to top it off, my mother left my dad and moved in with us for a while. She did this two more times before Bill told her flat out, "No more." He let her know that if she was going to leave her husband again, she needed to go someplace else.

Bill had our new place finished enough that we could move in the following spring. Now he could work on it while we lived there. This was helpful for all of us because we were able to be together as a family every evening. In addition, my anxiety attacks were becoming much more frequent and severe, so I needed help taking care of the family.

In the late 1940s and early 1950s, the medical profession lacked the diagnoses and treatments for mental illness that are available today. I was suffering from severe panic attacks that would come over me constantly each day. I would sweat profusely, have trouble breathing, and experience rapid heartbeat. To compound the problem, I was having these problems every day with two young children at home. The panic attacks progressed into a severe case of agoraphobia, and it became aggressively worse each year. I was rapidly developing a series of fears. I was afraid to go outside, afraid to be alone, afraid to go downstairs into our basement to do the laundry, and even afraid to shower for fear of being trapped inside of it. My life had become one big fear. It was literally a living hell for me.

As if my problems were not enough for us to handle, in the summer of 1954, Bill suddenly became very ill and started to lose weight rapidly. One day he was helping my Uncle Elmer pour the foundation for his new home when he became ravenously thirsty. He was drinking a half-gallon of water at a time, and it was doing nothing to quench his thirst. By the time he came home, his tongue and throat were so raw he could barely swallow. I immediately called a doctor and asked him what I should do. The doctor told me to bring him in first thing in the morning and to be sure that Bill did not fall asleep that night. Later I realized that if Bill had gone to sleep, he might not have woken up. I never understood why the doctor neglected to have me take Bill to the emergency room at the nearest hospital, but I listened to his orders and kept Bill awake by playing cards all night.

The next day, the doctor diagnosed Bill with diabetes. He lost 50 pounds in three weeks and was so weak he could not work. My husband was 30 years old, and I was told he would not likely reach the age of 40. To combat his prognosis, we decided to go to the library together and check out books on nutrition, diabetes, and anything related to eating. I studied these books and put Bill on a nourishing, balanced diet in conjunction with his insulin shots. It was not long before he started to regain some of his weight and strength. He never went back to a doctor for his diabetes but he remained healthy and took insulin shots twice a day for the rest of his life. After Bill recovered, he decided to go into business for himself as a mason contractor and did very well. Unfortunately, much of our income went to doctors who were still trying to figure out my health problems.

Bill and I were determined to ensure the girls would enjoy their young lives regardless of our health problems. If you asked them today about Ramsey, they would remember the good times and occasional days when daddy would tell them that mommy did not feel good. On really bad days, after the girls were old enough to be in school all day, I would accompany Bill to his job sites and sit in the truck all day while he worked. Our neighbor was very helpful and would watch the girls from 3 p.m. until 5 p.m. until we came home. I placed all of my confidence in Bill; if he was with me, I could struggle through food shopping, a picnic, or any activity we planned to do with the girls.

I soon realized I could no longer drive; it was just too dangerous for my family and me. The last time I drove was following a trip to the doctor's office. I was rather upset at the time, and he told me to keep driving or I would never drive again. I needed gas, so I was forced to stop at the gas station in town. I must have looked bad because the owner, who knew both of us quite well, called Bill and told him, "Mina is heading home and something is really wrong." I never remembered the drive home. I only remember being at the top of the hill leading to our house and seeing Bill frantically waving his hands while standing in the middle of the road. He said I was flying down the road, drove right up the side lawn, and narrowly missed a large apple tree in the yard. That was the last time I ever drove a car.

Bill was wonderful and supportive every day and tried to help me deal with my problems. Without hesitation, he took the girls to their scout meetings and school activities in the evenings. During the wintertime, when the pond across the street froze over, Bill would put up lights and we would all skate on the pond. Mina was a good skater, but Sandra was younger and fell down a lot, so I had to wrap her head in a heavy scarf to protect her.

Our two daughters were polar opposites from one another. Mina was independent and would try anything, but Sandra was timid and more of a mommy's girl. Mina had to excel at any endeavor she tried, but in contrast, Sandra would always stop and smell the roses, both figuratively and literally. On many occasions I was surprised with a bouquet of flowers that Sandra had picked on her way home from school. As she walked home she found rhododendrons, peonies, or many other pretty flowers along the way. Unfortunately, she found them growing in other people's flower gardens. Quite a few times I received irate phone calls from neighbors asking me to keep our little girl out of their flowerbeds. When I tried to explain to Sandra why she should not do this, she would tell me, "Mommy, the flowers were so pretty I wanted to pick some for you."

Since this was a time long before the Internet and television was in its infancy, our children grew up quite naïve. One of our biggest laughs was when the girls became occupied with a small watering hole next to our place. It was less than 10 feet across and, at most, it was a foot deep. One day they were both busy out there for hours. When they came home, they told us with much excitement about all of the little frogs that were sitting in the water. They told us all of the frogs were stuck together so they took the time to pull them apart one by one. Those poor frogs must have been having such a good time before my kids found them.

Mina was definitely the more independent child. When she came up with an idea, good or bad, Bill usually left her alone to learn the hard way. Of course, Bill watched from a distance to make sure she did not hurt herself in the process. One of my favorite stories of her stubbornness was when she decided she wanted to be Huck Finn and set out to make a raft by herself and float away on the pond across the street. Lucky for us, the pond was all of 2 feet deep. She did a nice job making the top of the raft, and then she put old oilcans underneath to keep it afloat. The plan was working so far except for the fact that when she nailed the cans to the bottom of the raft, she did not realize she was puncturing the cans and thereby causing them to fill up with water. Off she went with her dad, dragging the raft over to the pond. He stayed at the edge to watch the outcome. She floated off, pulling herself along with her dreams, when slowly the raft started to sink. She was yelling, "Daddy do something!" He yelled back that he was unable to help her since the cans were filling with water and the raft was going to sink. Of course, after the raft reached the bottom of the pond, Mina was barely knee deep in water so we were not too concerned about her going down with the ship. However, we did have to deal with a very dejected little girl who learned a lesson about both physics and listening to her father.

At Christmas, Bill and the girls decorated the outside of our house. They did such a wonderful job that we even took first prize in our neighborhood contest one year. The girls always wanted to help Bill. They often wanted to follow their father up onto the roof to help him work. Since he did not have any safety harnesses for the girls, he did the next best thing – he nailed their slacks to the roof so they would not fall but could still hand him things and help out. This is how we tried to live a normal life under abnormal conditions. Today, this would probably be looked upon as child abuse.

The girls also enjoyed camping at Bear Mountain, the same place where Bill and I used to picnic before we were married. They had wooden platforms where we set up our tents for the evening. On one of our outings, we were lucky enough to spend the night underneath the tail end of a hurricane. Poor Bill spent the whole night tightening and then loosening the tent ropes to keep the tent in one piece. We made it through the night, but we did not get much sleep.

Every year right after Christmas, the weather was too cold for mason work so Bill was home for a few weeks. He used this time for projects around our house, like knocking out a wall, setting the entire kitchen in brick, or even adding an addition to the house. By the time we sold it, we had a very nice house to offer.

After I became homebound, we spent our time playing board games, building with Lincoln logs or tinker toys, and having tea parties. The girls loved it when the three of us played dress-up and waited for daddy to come home. Our dress-up ranged from Indians in war paint to fancy gowns and make-up. I rarely had a full-blown panic attack when I was with Bill. If one came on when I was alone with the girls, I went into the bathroom and waited for it to subside. When it was over, I would come out and tell them I had a bellyache and needed to lie down for a while.

One Sunday I was having a particularly hard time. To keep the girls from noticing, Bill had a brainstorm. He said, "Let's give Mommy an egg shampoo." I still remember it like it was yesterday. Bill put towels on the floor and sat me down with my back resting against a chair, and the three of them cracked a bunch of eggs on top of my head and rubbed them into my hair. The kids had a ball and it lightened my mood as well. Of course, later on Bill was kind enough to shampoo the mess out of my hair.

By now we had been living with my problems for almost 10 years. The doctors finally told Bill that they could not help me, and they suggested I be placed in a sanitarium. His answer was, "Like hell I will." Obviously I had my problems, and to compound the issue, Bill's sugar level would get to the point where it would dramatically rise and fall inside of a few minutes. We were told he had a catalyst in his system that stored the insulin and then let it out. When it let out, the drop in his blood sugar would send him into convulsions. I could see it coming on, and I would immediately give him some cookies to prevent him from going into shock. I followed Bill to his job sites not only because of my condition but also because I was terribly worried about his health every day. We came to the conclusion that this was no way to live our life. We needed to find a solution that would both fit our lifestyle and conquer our problems.

We knew how to keep Bill's diabetes in check, so our next plan was to figure out how to deal with my problems. We decided that if we could find a way to be together all day without hindering Bill's work and the children's lives, we could beat this. I could monitor Bill's blood sugar level, and at the same time he would be by my side. If I had those types of reassurances each day, I felt I could do much better.

In 1959, we devised a plan. We decided to sell everything in New Jersey, including the business he worked so hard to develop and the home that he built for us. It did not bother either one of us because to us they were simply material possessions that could easily be replaced. Our happiness together was more important. We made a nice profit on the house and used the money to purchase a dairy farm in Pennsylvania where the four of us could work together and be together every day. Keep in mind that our health problems were never cured. We just found a way to live in spite of them. It was the best move we could have made for both our marriage and our family. We decided we would take care of each other and have a good time doing it. Tragically, many cases like mine end up in divorce, or even worse, suicide. How lucky I was to have a husband who stuck by me the way that Bill did, someone who was willing to do whatever it took for us to have a memorable and loving life.

Our Wedding Photo
March 21, 1943

My attic room in Jacksonville, FL

Bill chopping up the porch in Atlantic, NC

Truck box we lived in, Beaufort, NC

Washing clothes in Nettie's yard, Beaufort NC

Aunt Jimmy

Bill getting ready to ring rooster's neck in Kingston, NC

Marine Base in Newport, Arkansas

Marine Base on Eniwetok

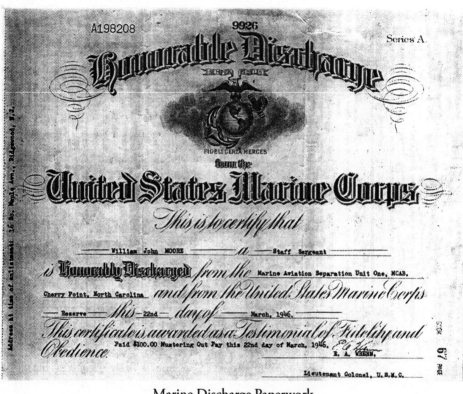

Marine Discharge Paperwork

BOOK 67 PAGE 92

Enlisted at _____ RS, New York, N.Y. _____ on the 24th day of November 19.43 to serve Dur. N.E. years
Born 1 October, 1923 at Southington, Conn.
When enlisted was (Date) 70 inches high, with Brown eyes, Brown hair, complexion: Ruddy citizenship: U.S.
Previous service: None.

Rank and type of warrant at time of discharge: Staff Sergeant-Aviation Temp. 21Jul44.
Weapons qualification: Rifle Sharpshooter - score of 299, 15Jan43.

Special military qualifications: Mechanic, aviation - SSN 747.

Service (sea and foreign): Central Pacific Area from 15 January, 1945 to 26 November, 1945.

Wounds received in service: None.
Battles, engagements, skirmishes, expeditions: None.

Remarks: Authority for discharge: Art. 3-15, MCM. Issued Certificate of Satisfactory Service; issued 2 patches, khaki, 2 patches, green, honorable service; issued honorable service and USMC honorable discharge buttons. Awarded Good-Conduct Medal 23Nov45. No offenses since that date.
Character of service excellent. R. C. Hammond, Jr.
Serial number 502598 R. C. HAMMOND, Jr., Major, U.S.M.C.

Is physically qualified for discharge. Requires neither treatment nor hospitalization.
I certify that this is the actual print of the right index finger of the man herein mentioned. _____ U.S.N. and Medical Officer.

Monthly rate of pay when discharged $100.80
I hereby certify that the within named man has been furnished travel allowance at the rate of 5 cents per mile from Cherry Point, N.C. to New York, N.Y. and paid $ 142.64 in full to date of discharge. Paid $ 29.70 travel allowance.

R. C. Hammond, Jr.
William John Moore R. C. HAMMOND, Jr., Major, U.S.M.C.
(Signature of man.) Commanding Officer.

Marine Discharge Paperwork

Bill Haessner (My Brother) in Army uniform during World War II

Mina helping her father build our house in Ramsey, NJ

Sandra and Mina clowning around

Our trip to the beach in Atlantic City, NJ

Farmhouse in Hop Bottom, Pennsylvania

The family farm with its new edition

Our Yamaha motorcycle we used to tour the country

Our security job and home in Las Vegas

50th Wedding Anniversary

My 70th birthday surprise in Las Vegas

Our blind dog Sweetie

Special Olympics basketball team in Las Vegas

My home in Forest City, Pennsylvania

Kitty lounging around

My dog Rosie

Chapter 8
LIFE ON THE FARM

Before we purchased the farm and moved to Pennsylvania, we wanted the girls to have a nice weekend at the shore. We knew that as soon as we moved to the farm our lives would consist of seven day work weeks without vacations. Although just the thought of the trip caused my heart to race, I had to grit my teeth and control my problems for the sake of the kids. We headed down to Atlantic City where Bill found a nice hotel and rented two rooms on the second floor so the girls could have a room next to ours. In the evening we sat out on the balcony and watched the waves roll onto the shore. We could not get over our two little girls sitting like queens on their own balcony, giggling every time they looked at us next door. It was a tough decision to move from our hometown, but we knew we were making the right choice to keep our family intact.

The next day at the ocean I had a little accident. A wave came in and knocked me for a loop. When I came up for air, I realized my front bridgework had been knocked out by the wave. Bill and I had a good laugh over it, but the girls were horrified with the way I looked with a missing front tooth. In the evening when we went out for dinner, my children tried to find a table where my back would be to the patrons so I could not face anyone. They were so embarrassed, but there was nothing I could do about it except keep my mouth shut. Regardless of the incident, we had a nice three-day vacation. Our rest on the shore needed to last us for a long time. The kids were old enough to swim in the ocean, and they had a great time bouncing around in the waves. Since this was long before any media hype on the dangers of shark attacks and almost 20 years before the movie "Jaws," we all dove into the ocean without any fear. We rode bicycles down the boardwalk, and the girls bought souvenirs at the Mr. Peanut Shop. They kick themselves for no longer having those souvenirs because they would be worth quite a bit on E-Bay today. Of course we can all look back on those things we bought for a couple of dollars in the 1950s – Grandma's old rocker, the children's Betsy-Wetsy dolls, flexible flyer sleds – and be amazed by what they would be worth today.

As soon as we returned from the shore, I made an emergency visit to the dentist to fix my front tooth. As soon as my tooth was fixed, we were off to begin our adventure in Pennsylvania. We searched the local New York newspaper and found real estate listings for farms for sale around Susquehanna County in northeastern Pennsylvania. The area was about three hours from our home in New Jersey, and we spent three weekends looking for farms. We contacted a local real estate agent from Nicholson, Pennsylvania, who had listed some of the farms in the paper. We had no idea what to look for in a dairy farm; we just followed our gut feeling. By the third weekend, none of the farms looked quite right to us yet. The realtor took us up a very long hill right outside the town of Nicholson, a nice, friendly, country town of around 2,000 people. When we reached the crest, we could see rolling hills dotted with farms with five mountaintops in the background. It looked like a setting from a beautiful painting. Off in the distance, we could see a red house with a small barn sitting on the top of a hill. When we drove a little closer, we saw that the home could use some paint, but the girls and I looked at each other, all hoping this was the farm for sale. The realtor made our day by turning into the horseshoe driveway of this house. The barn was small, but Bill said we could easily build a larger one. The lot consisted of 100 acres total, including

15 acres of woodlands that bordered fields for crops and pastures for grazing cattle. There was even a creek running through the property.

When we saw the farm the current owners, the Curottos, had only 10 milking cows in the barn. We knew right away we needed quite a few more cows to earn a living. The house was also really dirty inside, and we found lots of mice running around. But it had a coal furnace for heat, along with a kitchen, dining room, front room, and a small downstairs bedroom and bath. Upstairs were three additional bedrooms. We never knew exactly how old the house was, but we joked that it was so old that George Washington may have slept there.

The front of the house had a porch with a slanted floor. Along the side porch that faced the road, the owners had planted a lilac bush and a beautiful maple tree, both of which had grown considerably over the years. After looking everything over, we told the owners we would buy it. With the land, the house, and the barn included, we purchased the property for $15,000. The realtor then drove us back to get our car, and we headed right back to talk to the owners. They were thrilled to sell the home because they wanted to return to their hometown in Vermont as soon as possible. Much to our benefit, this made them very open to any of our suggestions.

In July of 1959, we started to make our move to Pennsylvania. Luckily we sold our home in New Jersey in less than a month for $25,000, so we were able to purchase the farm free and clear, with some money to spare. We packed everything up in New Jersey, and Bill made the six-hour round trip to the farm every day with his truck filled with our belongings. We made an agreement with the Curottos to move our belongings in immediately and use the empty front room of the house for storage. By the end of the week, we were completely moved out of New Jersey. As soon as we moved everything from our home in New Jersey, we pitched a tent by the maple tree outside and began our farming life. We were going to be apprentices for a little while and live side by side with the Curottos while they taught us about farming. I will never forget our first night at the farm. Bill, Sandra, Mina, and I laid on the grass by the maple tree and dreamed. Bill said to me once, "After we move here, remember I'll always be next to you to help you. I won't ever try to push you. It will be up to you to decide if you are ready to try something." It was a slow but rewarding process, and in a few years the severe panic attacks subsided but I still needed Bill close to me. I always knew I could depend on him completely.

We paid cash for the farm so it was only a matter of days before the electricity, phone, and farm were all in our name. The rest of the plan did not work out quite as well. The fieldwork was already done so they neglected to show us how most of the equipment worked. Bill watched them milk the cows a couple of times and did his best to quickly learn how to clean the milking machines, but that was about the extent of the tutorial. Most of the time, the Curottos were gone, and we had no idea where they went. In our minds, we were enjoying our camping vacation before the real work started on the house.

At the start of our second week on the farm, we woke up in our tent to find a big surprise: The family had literally run off in the middle of the night. We soon found out that one of the reasons for their quick disappearance was that the well on the property had run dry. The cows were out to pasture, so they could drink out of the pond, but the calves had to stay in the barn. They were mooing so loudly for water that we could barely hear ourselves think. Our only option was to bring water from the pond to the young stock. We took the milk cans normally used for shipping milk to the creamery and used them to haul water up from the pond. Each calf could easily drink a couple of gallons of water per sitting, so we had to run down to the pond on the tractor a couple of times each day.

We immediately called a well driller who started that day. By the end of the week we had great water. He hit an underground creek, and we could actually hear the water rushing by if we were standing close enough to the well pipe. We now had plenty of water for the animals and for ourselves to drink, bathe, and even do laundry. However, since we sold our washing machine with our previous house, I was forced to go back to doing laundry by hand in the bathtub for a while. Luckily I was quite well trained from washing clothes while following Bill around in the Marine Corps, so I was quite adept at the art of hand washing.

After we took care of the calves, we were now ready to try and milk the cows. We had no idea how to call them in from the fields, but luckily when we opened the door, the cows were all standing outside the barn door waiting to come in and be milked. We opened the door and prayed. We could not believe what happened next. The cows came in nicely, one by one, and each went into their respective stall. We hooked them all up, and Bill half-jokingly explained to the cows that he had no idea what he was doing and if they could be so kind as to cooperate, it would really help us out. Bill did just fine, and since we only had 10 cows to milk, it did not take too long. Part of the never ending joy of farming included required milkings twice a day, seven days a week, including holidays. When we first started, it took us about three hours to feed the cows and calves, milk the cows, and clean up the barn and equipment afterwards. This would occur each morning and evening. It did not take us too long before we were efficient enough to add 15 additional cows to the fold and still be able to complete all of our work in the same three hours of time.

We were proud of ourselves for figuring out the milking equipment on our own, so I thought I would head to the house until the evening milking while Bill shoveled the manure out of the barn. How wrong we were. One of the cows named Maggie was just a little ways from the barn, and she starting acting strangely. It would have been helpful if we had known she was pregnant, but much to our surprise, she started to give birth to a calf. We decided she probably knew a lot more about it then we did, so we just left her alone and watched from a short distance. She did fine and delivered a large, healthy calf. We thought that adventure was over, but then we discovered that cows also have to deliver their afterbirth, and we had no idea what to do with it. The poor cow was walking around dragging this big thing behind her. Bill quickly thought that if he stepped on it when she walked past, it would simply flip out on the ground behind her. However, Bill did not take into account how slippery the afterbirth was, so instead of stepping on it, his foot slipped off and he wound up on his behind. We quickly decided that Maggie knew best how to handle this situation, so we let her have at it.

While all of the cows were out in the field, Maggie's calf, which was a bull, stayed right by her side and nursed throughout the day. When the cows came in for their evening milking, Maggie walked into the barn and her calf followed. We put the calf in a calf pen, which was sad for us because Maggie stood there mooing for her. One of the other parts to the birthing process we quickly learned was to milk the colostrums out of the mother for three days and feed it to the calf. It was very obvious because it did not look like anything we would ever consider drinking, but it contained everything the calf needed to be healthy.

All of this happened during our first day as farmers, so we were getting quickly initiated into farming life. We knew that if we could handle that first day without losing it that we had a really good chance of making it as farmers. The next day after milking, Bill decided to tackle the barn since it was a complete mess. It was so dirty and disheveled that he had to actually scrape manure off the walls. The girls and I helped out by tackling the house, which was not in much better shape than the barn. It took quite a few hours of hot water, soap, and scrubbing brushes to take care of it. By the end of the week we had a nice clean barn and house. We also had to set mousetraps all over the house to rid our home of mice. The barn did not have a problem with mice because several barn cats were left behind and they kept the barn under control.

When we started, our only source of income was from selling milk to the creamery at approximately $5 per 100 pounds of milk, or 5 cents per pound. The creamery was located a few miles down the road in Hop Bottom, and they paid us on the 25th day of each month for our product. When we first started, we delivered the milk each day in a can that held roughly 85 pounds, so we had the potential to earn $4.25 per can. Because the farm had six milk cans in the barn, we assumed that all of them were going to the creamery full each day, and Bill originally based his budget on them. After the first day, he quickly realized how much work we had to do around the farm. On the first morning, he only filled two cans full of milk. He was so concerned that he asked one of the neighbors if he was doing something wrong and not getting all of the milk out of cows. Our new neighbor chuckled and assured him he was doing everything correctly, however the Corrutos did not like to lift the full cans so they used several additional milk cans to lighten the load. This really put a damper on the family budget until we could bring in more cows.

One of the few bright spots in the farming equipment was the International tractor, which was called an "H." It worked like a charm. When Bill went out to spread manure on the hay fields, I stood on the back of the tractor and went with him. It took a few months before I was self-confident enough to let him go without me, but I still watched him from the barn. I felt really good when he said he liked it better when I came with him. Our neighbors probably thought that we were crazy going out on the tractor spreading manure together. We never discussed our reason with our neighbors who I am sure wondered why I could not let my husband even work out in the fields alone. Our problems were kept in the family. They never did know why.

The following week, Bill started to build the new barn because it had to be done by spring. We needed room for more cows and a bigger hayloft to store the hay for our herd. We built a barn big enough to house 35 Holstein cows for milking as well as 10 young calves. Our days were spent working on the new barn. The girls and I hauled block and mixed cement while Bill put up the foundation and block walls. We finished that part by the time the girls had to start school. Sandra went to sixth grade in a little one-room schoolhouse in the town of Hop Bottom. It was perfect for her because she was shy and would rather be at home than anywhere else. Hop Bottom consisted of a bank, food store, hardware store, funeral home, and gas station. Mina was in high school and had to ride the bus for about a half-hour to get to school. That year, the school district had opened up a new high school that consolidated all of the little neighboring town high schools into one. This was perfect for Mina because she was more adventurous and eager to be involved in the first class at a big new school.

When school started, our help was gone, so Bill and I had to establish a working routine. We kept this same routine the entire time we owned the farm. Bill and I got up at 5 a.m. and had a big breakfast. Many farmers in the area did not eat breakfast until after the first milking, but we needed to eat first to keep Bill's diabetes in check. After breakfast we would go out and milk the cows together. The girls got up later, dressed for school, made their own breakfasts, packed their lunches, and went off to school. After milking, I cleaned the milk machine while Bill led the cows out into the barnyard. Although a farm may appear to be dirty, we quickly learned that we constantly had to clean all of the milking equipment. The local creamery sent inspectors out to the farms to make sure the product they purchased was up to par. If the inspectors did not pass our farm and equipment, we would lose our only source of income because we would have no other place to sell our milk. I never particularly liked this part of the job. The equipment was extremely awkward to handle as well as quite heavy to move around, but it had to be done.

After we let the cows out to pasture, we went back in the house for a second cup of coffee and watched the cows for awhile. I will explain later why this is necessary. Bill then went out to clean the barn while I did my household chores such as laundry, ironing, and making desserts. Next, we would deliver the milk to the creamery a few miles down the road in Hop Bottom.

We did field work after lunch in the spring, summer, and fall. In the winter we worked on equipment, handled cold weather problems in the barn, and plowed the snow when it fell. Our location on top of the hill was beautiful, but the snowdrifts were a problem because every day, even when it was snowing, the milk had to be taken to the creamery. Our neighbor farmed with horses, so when the snow drifts were impossible, he would take our milk tanks on a horse drawn sleigh across the fields.

When the girls came home from school they did their homework while I made supper. We ate dinner promptly at 5 p.m. It was our steadfast rule that all work stopped at suppertime regardless, and we all sat down for a relaxing supper. Our day was discussed, and if we had any problems, we tried to solve them. Mostly we shared many laughs and much love. Our kids were at a mischievous age. If one of us asked Mina to pass the potatoes, she was likely to pass them overhand. On more than one occasion, this led to a food fight. After dinner Bill and I headed out to the barn for the 6 p.m. milking while the girls did the dishes and cleaned up the kitchen. We were usually able to complete the evening milking by 8 p.m.

We enjoyed the rest of the evening any way we liked. Sometimes Mina would make us a delicious pie, or we made caramels or cookies together, or we just watched television as a family. We did not have the girls help out in the barn. We did not want them smelling like cows when they headed off for school. On the weekends, the girls used Saturdays as their own time and would help in the barn on Sundays by brushing the cows and helping to keep them nice and clean. In the winter months they would help out with clipping the cows. Mina liked the machinery, so she learned to handle all of the equipment really well. Sandra also liked the cows and the barn so our lifestyle worked out for both children.

Now that we were beginning to understand the milking process, our next task was to develop a feeding system to help the cows produce more milk. We did not have any books on how to run a farm, so we gathered any available information from the people who ran the local feed store and from our veterinarian. We knew that anything we learned about farming would make this profession more profitable for us in the long run.

Earlier I mentioned that we used to sit and watch the cows after we went inside for our second cup of coffee. To understand this ritual requires a little bit of knowledge about the nature of cows. This paragraph alone is about 100 percent more information than we started with on the farm. Right after a cow delivers a calf, it produces more milk than at any other time of the year. Three months after the cow gives birth, it goes into heat, signaling that it is once again time for it to breed. The cow can still be milked during its first six months of pregnancy, but the amount of milk it produces gradually decreases each month. During the last three months, the cow is "dried off" and does not give any milk until the calf is born. This cycle means that a cow can produce a calf once a year while providing milk for nine out of 12 months.

We of course did not have any of this information. Three months after Maggie gave birth there was a big commotion in the pasture. All of the cows were getting restless, and some of the cows were jumping on the backs of the other cows. In addition, they were taking turns sniffing each other's rear ends. Since all of the cows were female, I was baffled by the situation, so I called the vet and told him I thought we might have a problem. I told him that for all I knew we might have a herd of lesbian cows because they were all females and all trying to ride each other. After the vet was able to finally control his laughter, he explained to me that the cow at the bottom of the commotion was the one in heat. He tactfully informed me that we should call the inseminator and have the cow bred.

We did not know the first thing about breeding cows. We also did not know that we should never keep a bull on the farm because they can be dangerous and unpredictable, especially when the cows are in heat. We just thought it was a coincidence that all of the cows were female when we took over the farm. We learned that when our cows had calves we were supposed to keep the heifers (females) so they could grow up to be milkers, and the bulls were to be raised for veal or slaughtered at the slaughter house. Later on, Bill had quite a time trying to explain to the girls and me that we could not keep Maggie's bull as a pet. The three of us were crying our eyes out when we took it to the slaughterhouse.

I called the inseminator and we learned everything we needed to know about breeding. We now understood why we left the cows in the barnyard for a half-hour every day before leading them out to pasture or back to the barn in the winter; it was to determine whether any of the cows were in heat. Our farming education was falling into place. I must admit it was much more of an adventure to learn on the fly than to know it all from the start.

After we had the cows handled, we needed to tackle the expansion of the barn. Bill and I were working very hard together, but the most difficult task was putting up the rafters by ourselves. The girls helped out by nailing the ceiling of the barn, which also served as the hayloft floor. The girls worked so hard at it that their wrists could hardly move by the end of each day.

We could not do much work from December through February because it was too cold and snowy. In March, our hearts were broken when a hefty late winter storm blew down all of the rafters we had worked so hard to erect. I think Bill could have cried at the sight of all of those lost hours of work. Bill was unaware of my plan, but I wrote to one of our former neighbors in Ramsey and told him about the many different people Bill helped in the past by working on their homes free of charge when we lived in the area. I asked if some of those people would be willing to help us out now. The first nice weekend in springtime, one car after another pulled into our driveway loaded with help. Bill could not believe I had set this entire thing up without his knowledge. In two days they had all of the rafters back up and supported in their final position. I fed our guests and did the farm work while the men worked on the barn. The guys were in stitches when they saw me take off on the tractor to spread the manure out in the pasture. The girls and my father kept the men supplied with nails and tools and water. At night, they slept wherever they found a spot on the floor. When they left they were a happy bunch of guys, and we were certainly more than appreciative. We were speechless and had no idea how we could ever properly thank everyone for their kindness and generosity. All of the men said the same thing to us. They remembered how many times Bill had helped them out, so they were more than happy to repay the favor.

Now that the rafters were up, we had about two months to get the aluminum roof on the barn before we had to start haying the fields. I was scared to death of the work Bill was doing on the roof. We had 200 sheets of aluminum roofing that needed to be attached and each measured 15 feet by 2.5 feet. We both knew Bill would get nowhere if he had to climb down for each sheet. Instead I had to get the sheets to him by climbing up the ladder along the rafters and handing him one sheet at a time as he nailed them to the rafters. When the wind blew, I had to really hang on to the sheets so they did not take me away like I was holding onto a sail. Bill encouraged me all the way, and as scared as I felt, I knew I had to do it. We got the job done just in time for the haying to start. When we were down to the last sheet, I broke down and cried my head off, so Bill came down, gave me a big hug, and took the last sheet up on his own. It was a big accomplishment for the entire family.

Even after the hay was moved, bailed, and stacked in the barn, we still were not finished with it. After we completed the hayloft upstairs, our next steps were to pour a concrete floor, put in new stall drinking cups for the cows, and install electric wiring. Bill's new toy in the barn was an automatic barn cleaner so we no longer had to shovel out the manure gutters. After all of the construction was completed, we were finally ready for more cows.

After the barn was finished, we spent the summer working in the fields where we grew corn, oats, and hay for the cows. It took much of the summer to mow and bale the hay to feed the cows for an entire year. We had two growing seasons for hay during the summer and if we were lucky, a third. To keep the cows fed, we produced 7,000 bales of hay each summer, along with the corn and oats.

After the fieldwork was done and the summer faded into fall and then winter, farming became a whole different story. Luckily, even in the winter, the barn was warm enough from the body heat of the cows that we only needed to wear a sweatshirt. As a matter of fact, the cows produced so much heat that we needed to run a very large window fan day and night to keep the dampness down. It was strange to go out to the barn early on a midwinter morning and chop the door free of ice, only to get in and find it relatively warm inside. It used to get so cold on our mountain that when we let the cows into the barnyard for a half-hour in the morning, we sometimes had to chop the door loose again just to get back inside.

Part of the barn cleaner extended outside over the manure spreader and had to be freed from ice on many mornings in order to clean the barn. The cold weather made much of our equipment operate on the brittle side, including the manure spreader. Every time it broke down we had to empty it by hand in order to fix it. The silage in the silo would also freeze a good 6 inches down, causing the silage conveyor not to work. Even in the face of all of these setbacks, we still had to drive to the creamery each day with the milk. This became especially challenging when our road was filled with up to 12 inches of snow after a storm.

Much like people cramped into an office or school during the winter, when it was too cold to go outside, our cows would often get sick. One year we had a barn full of cows with pneumonia. We were in the barn for days, taking temperatures and giving penicillin shots. Luckily we did not lose any cows, but we did lose plenty of milk because we were not allowed to ship milk from cows for three days following a penicillin shot.

I can honestly say that there are more ways for farmers to lose money than to make money. When we first started, we were lucky to make $300 a month in milk revenue. This was hardly enough to cover the bills, let alone put towards farm equipment or upgrades. It took us several years before were we even able to make enough money to pay into Social Security for our future retirement.

One day we walked into the barn and saw that the cows had large bumps the size of ping-pong balls all over their backs. Bill and I wondered what in the world they had been exposed to, and we worried it could be measles. I called our local vet to come out and look over the cows, and he assured me that they did not have measles or any other type of sickness for that matter. Instead, we learned that flies bite at the cows hooves in the summer and actually deposit eggs. The eggs travel through their internal system and later emerge on their backs in the form of a grub that produces many flies. This is one of the many wonderful things we learned during our first year of farming.

All in all, our cows were also a lot of fun, and we enjoyed our daily routine. Maggie was an excellent milker. She could squirt a stream of milk clear across the barn. When Bill got ready to milk her, our Momma Cat (we had many cats around the farm that just appeared) came running, sat in the walkway, and waited for Bill to squirt milk into her mouth. She sat up on her hind legs, drinking away. Two of our cows, Virginia and Kathy, always waited patiently for me to come and milk them. When I got between them, they would squeeze together and not let me out. They never hurt me; they would playfully squeeze together just enough to trap me. I would have to call to Bill, and he would holler, "Let mommy out!" and they would separate. I know many farmers would not believe this, but it is true. Our cows were our friends. The vet once told us that our farm was the only place he did not need to use nose leads on the cows when drawing blood for tests. I would just hold each cow by the head and talk to it, telling it that everything was going to be okay. Bill did not like it when I held the cows during the shots because he was always afraid one would send my flying, but they never did.

Nellie, our oldest cow and a real sweetheart, came in one time with her eye practically hanging out of its socket. We never figured out how it happened. I took a coffee cup and filled it with warm water and boric acid, and Bill pushed her eye back into place. I then set the cup over her eye and picked up her head to allow the water to bathe her eye. I did this several times a day, and she never fought me. It must have felt soothing. Her eye never got infected, but unfortunately, she lost her sight in that eye.

About five years after we moved to the farm, the rules changed on how to store milk. Farmers were required to install refrigerated bulk tanks to store milk for two days, and a tanker truck would pick up the milk every other day. The good news was that we no longer had to deliver the milk to the creamery ourselves, which was three miles from our farm. The bad news was that all of the farmers now had to build big new milk houses to accommodate the bulk tank. The tank we purchased held 360 gallons. It also gave us one more item that had to be cleaned thoroughly.

One day I decided I needed new glasses to help me with my work in the house and the barn, and it turned out to be a day to remember. The doctor talked me into bifocals, but I was not really crazy about the idea. I wore them all day trying to get used to looking through the two different areas on the lenses. Not long after I entered the barn to start milking the cows, it happened. I looked down to step over the gutter, and I stepped no where near where I intended to step. I tripped, completely lost my balance, and landed in the gutter, completely covering myself with manure. I walked up to the house where the girls were doing the dishes. I do not think I ever heard them laugh as hard as when they saw me. Into the tub I went, and when I returned to the barn it was without my glasses. I decided I could live without bifocals after that day.

When Sandra started her sophomore year in high school she decided she wanted to learn how to sew. Mina worked at a camp during the summer, and she used her money to buy Sandra a sewing machine for Christmas. She swore she could teach herself; all she needed was the material, thread, and a pattern to follow. I could not argue with her because whenever I wanted to learn something new I just bought instructions and followed them very successfully. We asked her what she wanted to make on her first try. I almost fainted when she said "a camel hair coat and hat to match." Bill just looked at me and said, "A coat it is." I cringed at the cost of the material for her first project, especially since I assumed most of the material would end up in the trash. However, when she completed the ensemble, it was beautiful and looked like it had come right off of a department store rack. She was even asked to be in a fashion show wearing her outfit. We all benefited from her sewing. One year she made me a new dress for Christmas. It was so pretty, I cried. On Mina's senior class trip, she was dressed to kill. We dug into my hope chest and retrieved all of my old clothes from New Jersey that I never wore on the farm, and Sandra made Mina a new wardrobe for her trip to Washington, D.C.

Bill decided he needed some type of activity away from the farm during the winter months so he joined the local bowling league. I thought it a great idea for him to have a little recreation. Our bowling alley consisted of two lanes in what used to be an old chicken coop in the town of Hop Bottom, Pennsylvania. Naturally I went along with Bill, which I was a little skeptical of doing at first. He felt it was no problem to bring his wife along, and he told me, "I bet some of the guys wished their wives could come." It turned out to be a lot of fun for both of us. The guys would all take turns sitting next to me to talk about their little problems. Since it was a small town and every one pretty much knew everyone else's business, I was probably the only person they could turn to for an unbiased female opinion. Bill really had the evening to himself because he rarely got a chance to sit by me. I became very good friends with the entire crew, and I gave them some good laughs with my farming stories.

We spent four years as a part of the bowling league. We both enjoyed the evening out and away from the farm. Luckily nothing bad ever happened around the farm when we were gone for a few hours, although the closest we ever came to a disaster in our home occurred one night while we were bowling. (This was after the girls were married and moved out.) There was a horrible thunderstorm, and lightning actually struck our house. Most of the windows downstairs were shattered and spewed glass all over the house. When we opened the front door, our beagle, Candy, flew out of the house and we could not find her. A week later she wandered in very hungry, but at least she was back.

Just like in New Jersey, every Christmas was a wonderful time of year around the farm. We made a paper chain each year – a tradition we started when the girls were young. By the time we were finished, it was so long that it covered the walls around a couple of rooms, draping from the ceiling. One of the advantages of living in the country was going to the woods to cut down our own Christmas tree. We always carried it back to the house as a family. One year the girls wanted to take the tractor by themselves to get our tree. We could not believe the tree they brought home. It spread out so far in our front room that it only left a small walkway to get upstairs. It was the most impressive Christmas tree we ever had.

To add to the festivities, we of course decorated a tree in the barn for the cows each year. They sure looked it over. When the inseminator came for the cows, he jokingly said, "I should have known you would have a tree in the barn." We would give each cow an apple for Christmas, which they really enjoyed. My father once told me an old German myth that on New Year's Eve, cows were able to talk for one night. Curiosity got the best of me so I went out to check. I did not hear any talking going on, but they might have waited until I left.

Our gifts to one another were mostly things we made ourselves, like fudge, caramels, good cookies, crochet items, sewn items, or wreaths. Bill would always get one tool and I always received one piece of jewelry, but our best gifts were the IOUs. We gave each other many of these and we always used them. Bill would get IOUs such as a barn cleaning, a day's hay from the hay loft, a truck wash, or his favorite, a fresh baked apple pie. I would get a house cleaning, a calf feeding, a shampoo, a fancy dinner, or a back massage. We always bought the girls some clothes, but the rest were IOUs such as cleaning their rooms, a hayride with friends, or no dishwashing for a couple of days.

One year before Christmas, Mina started a new pattern that went on every night for a few weeks. When we came in from the barn, Mina was already up in her room and she did not come down for the rest of the evening. I let it go on for a few nights and then I reamed her. I wanted her to explain to me where she got the idea to go to her room instead of spending the evening with the family. She just stood there while I scolded her. The next night she was upstairs again, and I was fuming. Luckily Bill pulled me aside and told me to leave her alone because she was working on a Christmas gift. At Christmas, I was so ashamed that I had scolded her because she presented us with a beautiful nativity scene. She had taken the time each evening to painstakingly hand paint each piece, and then she would sneak them to school and fire them in the art room kiln to finish the pieces. The camels were about 18 inches tall, and everything else was proportionate. We had to put all of the leaves in the dining room table just to display it. Sandra was just as creative and secretive. I never saw a trace of any sewing when Sandra made me a dress for Christmas. They must have worked like beavers while I was in the barn. We honestly had such loving years together as a young family.

In the winter of 1962 we asked our neighbor, Al Shack, if he could take care of the farm for three days while we went back to New Jersey to visit our close friends, Babe and Mickey. We told Al we would be home in time to do the milking on the third night, but we hit a blizzard on the way back. To make matters worse, the morning had been exceptionally warm, so Al cracked open a couple of windows in the barn. By late afternoon it was snowing so hard and fast that Al figured he better get back over to our place to close the windows. Unfortunately, by the time he realized it, he could no longer reach our place because the snow was too high. As we were slowly making our way up the hill towards our farm, many of the power lines were down, and the power was out in every home we passed. The wind was like a cyclone, and it was snowing so hard we could hardly see in front of us. By some miracle, our car got us within a half mile of our house by 3 p.m., but the roads became completely impassible after that point. It was bitter cold outside, but we could not stay in car or hope for a snowplow to come by. We had no other option but to try and walk back to our house. To make matters worse, we were all dressed in our Sunday best returning from New Jersey. Bill pulled out our suitcase; we put our pajama bottoms over our legs and tied our pajama tops over our heads in addition to using anything else we could find to cover our hands and shoes. We headed out, and Bill walked first to make a path in the deep snow that was drifting across the road from the wind. Sandra held onto Bill. Mina was next, holding on to Sandra, and I brought up the rear. It was so cold and scary. Even though the girls were teenagers, at one point they told us they could not walk anymore because they were frozen stiff. Bill looked at both of the girls and hollered to just hang on and keep walking. Later he confided in me that the only reason he yelled at them so forcefully was because he was beginning to fear that we needed to keep walking or we would freeze to death.

Although it seemed like hours, it probably took us less than an hour to walk the half-mile back to our house. After feeling like we were going to freeze, we finally made it out of the wind and snow. The first thing we did when we arrived at the house was put on some really warm clothes. The howling wind had actually blown the front door open because it was never locked, and quite frankly we never had a need for a key. To make matters worse, the furnace had gone out. The house was so cold that our goldfish bowl was frozen solid.

We had no time to worry about the house because the cows were bellowing so loud that we could hear them through the storm. This could only mean one thing: They had run out of water. We all went out to the barn and immediately closed the windows to help the cows warm up the barn. Bill started thawing out their drinking cups with a blowtorch. Overall we were lucky because none of the pipes burst and the electricity came back on fairly quickly. As each drinking cup was thawed, one less cow was yelling for water. The girls fed the cows grain and hay. They were able to get water to the young livestock by the pail once Bill thawed out a faucet. It took us until midnight to get through the milking. None of us were cold anymore, but it was a hard way to warm up.

Next we headed back to the house to face our last set of problems. Bill started a fire in the furnace and I heated up a couple cans of soup for dinner. Our home was so cold we could have used it as an icehouse. When we were through with dinner we all grabbed the blankets from our beds and laid around the big floor register where the heat came up from the furnace. We thawed the goldfish out slowly in the oven, and they miraculously lived for many years. In the morning we all kind of wondered whether our vacation was worth it. If the girls mention that trip now they say, "Mom, we could have died wearing so little clothing in the blizzard." The only answer I can give them is, "We didn't." After that experience I learned my lesson and always kept a big bag filled with warm clothes, old boots, hats, and gloves in the car or truck until winter was over.

On another winter day, our farm completely iced over from a storm. All around us the ground was a clear sheet of ice and the trees were covered as well. It was picturesque and undisturbed because so few cars drove past our farm. We made the most of it, and the day turned out to be one of our most enjoyable afternoons. The area running from our big barn door to the bottom pasture was a long hill perfect for sleigh riding. What made it even more fun was not using a sleigh at all. The four of us just laid down on our bellies and away we went. What a thrill it was just flying down that hill on our own. The only problem was that we had to get back up the hill, which proved to be quite a challenge. Our solution to the problem was to pry a rock loose from a stonewall at the edge of the field and use it to break holes in the ice so we could climb back up the hill. If we lost our footing we would simply slide back down the hill and start all over again. I was very proud of myself because I was slowly inching my way up the hill without any help. Then I noticed my nasty family working their way towards me rather than moving up the hill. I could not believe my family thought it was okay to gang up on me, but apparently they thought I was fair game. When they reached me, two of them loosened my hands and the third gave my leg a tug, and I slid back down the hill. We were out there for hours having a wonderful time. Sometime later, the people on the farm behind us said they really had a laugh watching us on the ice hill. These are the types of moments with my family that I treasure the most. I always felt that the fun we made that did not cost us a penny was usually the most fun of all.

Mina graduated from high school in 1965, and the following year she married a local trucker she met shortly after high school. Sandra graduated in 1967 and married a farmer in 1969, which was what she wanted. We gave each of our daughters $200 towards their wedding. They each brought a wedding gown for around $100 and used the rest for flowers, a wedding cake, and their going away outfits. We held a family reception at our house for each child. For both weddings, Sandra made the maid of honor and bridesmaid gowns as well as my outfit. I was petrified when the usher walked me down the isle alone and I had to wait for what seemed like forever until Bill walked our daughter down the aisle and sat next to me. Since neither of the families our daughters married into knew anything about my health problems, they probably did not understand why we chose not to have larger receptions. There was no way I could have made all of the arrangements and handled all of the guests around me. The girls understood, and that really was all that mattered to us.

After a couple of years of marriage, Mina had a son, John, in 1968, followed by another son, Dan, in 1970. Sandra also had children a few years into her marriage. She gave birth to Eric in 1972, and a daughter, Julie, in 1974.

Bill and I continued to work the farm until 1974. The work finally got to be too much for us to handle alone without the girls around anymore. Working seven days a week on a farm, regardless of health or age, can become very exhausting. We met with our doctor, and he told us that the stress of running the farm by ourselves would eventually kill us. In addition, we were at a point where much of the equipment on the farm was getting old and needed to be replaced. If we purchased new equipment, we would have to spend years continuing to operate the farm just to pay back the loans. That evening we had a long talk about our future, and by bedtime we had already decided to put the farm up for sale.

The farm sold in two weeks and was purchased by the realtor that listed it. As soon as the house was sold, we contacted an auctioneer to set up an auction for our household items, the cows, and the farming equipment. It was a very strange to watch all of the items we collected over the years being sold right off of our front porch. We were disappointed when some of the most expensive furniture sold for next to nothing, but then we chuckled when old farm tools or a bucket of nails and bolts that we would have given away sold for 10 times their value.

We did not have a set amount of money in mind from the sales at the auction. We just hoped to have enough to purchase the items we wanted for the next stage of our life. We invested the money we made in certificates of deposit that paid 9 percent annually. With the money we made, we planned on living on a budget of $4,500 per year.

Bill and I always wanted to travel around the United States after we raised the girls. We used part of the money from the auction to purchase a camper and a pickup truck to fulfill this dream. Our children were not as excited about the decision as we were. They felt we should have stayed in Pennsylvania to be closer to our grandchildren. Bill and I felt differently about it. We did our very best to give our girls a loving family life. Since both of our daughters were married and had children of their own, in our minds it was their turn to do the best they could for their children. We felt it was our turn to get back to being a couple again and live for each other.

Regardless, we were off to see what adventures awaited us as we traveled around the country at our leisure.

Chapter 9
TRAVELING

Since the children were grown and on there own and we were able to sell the farm relatively easily, we set off to see the country. We traveled nonstop from 1974 to1984. Although we knew we wanted to see the entire country, our main goal was to experience the out-of-the-way areas this country had to offer. First we needed to figure out exactly what we needed for our journey. After looking over all of our options, we decided to purchase a camper, a pickup, and a small motorcycle. We chose the pickup and camper route over a Winnebago so we could have much more flexibility wherever we stopped. Instead of hauling the camper around, we would unhook at a campground and use the pickup or motorcycle to tour around the surrounding areas.

We kept our car, a 1972 Mercury Cougar, for a short time to use as a trade-in for the pickup. We decided to purchase a 35-foot-long Coachman camper from a dealership in New York. Luckily, when we arrived, the sales manager liked our car so much he made us an even trade for his 1-year-old Chevy 350 pickup. Even though Bill was more of a Ford man, he just could not pass up that deal. It was a smart move on our part since the pickup lasted the entire time we traveled.

Our next purchase was a motorcycle. We found a new 75-horsepower Kawasaki that was going to be perfect for little day trips wherever we set up camp. We started our travels during the height of the gas shortage in the early 1970s, so much like today we looked to save money on gas whenever possible. The camper and motorcycle combined cost us about $10,000. Since we made an even trade for the pickup, we started off in fairly good shape.

We did not have a set plan as to where we were going to travel, we only knew we wanted to be in the South during the winter and see the northern states during the summer months. This made it much easier to camp all year long, and the last thing we wanted to do was fight icy roads and snow while pulling a large camper. We wanted to visit each state and see as much of it as possible rather than going back to the same region more than once. This was the main reason we purchased the motorcycle. It was much easier to park the pickup and camper at a campground and use it as a base camp, then go off on the motorcycle for the day or longer.

As a result of the money we invested, we had about $4,000 per year available to us for traveling. We saved money by camping in national forests for free whenever possible, or we rented space at campgrounds for the entire month instead of by the week, which was always a big savings. In fact, many times it was cheaper to rent a spot for a month in a campground compared to a one-week rental. When we were low on money, we would either barter for services or stop and work for a while. Times were much different around the country, and people were not so reluctant to help strangers, unlike today. We held odd jobs such as pumping gas for two weeks in Jacksonville, Florida so the owners could go on a trip. The gas station was connected to a gift shop that we also watched. We actually stayed at their home with their four children for two weeks so the parents could go on their first vacation alone.

If we were really low on money, we simply stopped traveling for a short time and found a job where we could both work together for a couple of months. We found odd jobs in hotel laundries and laundromats, as campground maintenance, in a carnival, and as our old standby, as migrant fieldworkers harvesting crops. All of the jobs were short term, so we always looked at them as a fun way to earn enough money to make our next move. We did not have many actual possessions between the two of us, so it was always fairly easy to make all of the money we needed. The only clothes we owned were three pairs of jeans each, some t-shirts, a bathing suit each, two pairs of shorts, and two pairs of sneakers. What else did we need for riding around on a motorcycle?

Since our children were still living in Pennsylvania, we technically used it as a base camp. We used Sandy's address as our own for any mail we needed to receive. Whenever we were going to be in an area for a month or more, we would let her know the address of the town so she could send the mail to a general delivery post office. Although we were sort of nomads, we still needed to keep our vehicles registered and let the IRS and Social Security know we still existed. The only time this created a problem for us was when we had some difficulties trying to cash a check in a state where we did not have a bank account. Since this was many years before the advent of the ATM machine, we would have to negotiate with the banks in each state just to cash our checks so we could live. I think many of the people helped us because they were in awe of the way we were living our life, or maybe they assumed we were crazy and just wanted to get rid of us. But who cares, we were happy.

During the summer of 1974, we pulled into Sandra's farm with our new "home" and stayed by them for a while before hitting the road. After saying goodbye to our daughters and grandchildren, we pulled out of Pennsylvania in our camper to see what lay ahead for us on the many roads in this great country.

Our first trip was to Elkhart, Indiana, to tour the Coachmen's plant. The company provided anyone who purchased a Coachman Camper a tour of the facility. The campground where we stayed was a nice first surprise. On Saturday night they put on an outdoor program. A wide creek ran through the area with the audience on one side and the show on the other. The show was about the colonial times with the settlers living in a small village. Suddenly, off in the distance we heard drums beating, and down the creek the Indians came in their canoes. They were not friendly Indians so the settlement was wiped out. The way they did the show was very impressive and a great way for us to start our new experience. While staying at this campground I read in a magazine about the state parks in Michigan. We decided to head there next. This was the official start of our roles on the road, with Bill as the driver and me as the planning coordinator and navigator.

The state parks in Michigan were everything the magazine advertised. There were so many parks in the state we could literally leave early in the morning, arrive by noon at our destination, enjoy it for the rest of the day, and then head for another park the following day or stay longer right where we were. The camping fees were only a couple of dollars a night. We drove the entire length of Michigan – from south to north through the center of the state – and came down along the east side. One park had a virgin forest that was a thrill to hike through. Another had a huge wooden cross cut from a single tree, and we had to walk up at least 100 steps to get to it. We also visited many other parks that were surrounded by lakes where people played all types of water sports. The last park we stopped at featured all kinds of sports fields where everyone joined in and formed teams to play against one other. Bill had a ball playing baseball and football, but he ended up with lots of aches and pains that evening.

After traveling through Indiana and Michigan, we decided to head south after a brief stopover at Sandy's farm in Pennsylvania. We ended up spending our first three years traveling exclusively on the East Coast. This way we could see all of the East Coast states while at the same time accustoming ourselves as well as our family to the idea of not seeing each other for months at a time. This was helpful to our children and us as we began to make plans to see the western half of the United States, which would take us away for a much longer period.

After our stop in Pennsylvania, our next destination was Orange City, Florida. The park we found only cost us $50 a month, including utilities and use of the swimming pool and shuffleboard courts. As we soon found out, shuffleboard seemed like the official sport of Florida retirees. The courts were lit and many times we found ourselves out in the evening playing some pretty cutthroat games until as late as 2 a.m.

One nice surprise of this site was the view we had of the rockets taking off from Cape Canaveral, even though we were 80 miles away from the launch site. Naturally, for our next trip we decided to ride out to Cape Canaveral on our little motorcycle. The road leading out to the cape had large wet ditches on both sides where alligators would sun themselves. A 75-horsepower motorcycle does not have too much speed with two people on it so all I could do was smile nicely and say "nice alligator, nice gator" as we rode past them. By the time we got back to the park, our behinds were so sore we could not sit right for a while.

Another area we visited was the St. John's River, where manatees came in to swim and feed near a hot spring off of the river. Manatees can reach a length of 10 feet and weigh more than 1,000 pounds, but the poor things were constantly getting their backs cut up from the motorboats on the river. The boats also accidentally killed many of them each year. Manatees are so timid that anyone could go in and swim with them. I chose against getting quite that close, but we did rub their heads and backs from the boat, which they seemed to like.

After a month in Orange City we headed for Frog Creek Campground in Bradenton, Florida. This area is on the Gulf of Mexico at Terra Cela Bay, which is just south of St. Petersburg. We loved this area for the shells we collected on the beach. When the tide was out, we found all kinds of shells including conch, olive, elephant ears, angel wings, cat's eyes, and tigers. We spent many of our days gathering shells, and in the evenings I made souvenirs out of them. I made jewelry such as earrings and broaches, as well as nightlights and airplanes. I also learned how to make animals out of the various shapes, so I made elephants that I would dress in circus outfits, a band of frogs, and many others. We set up a table in front of our camper, and I sold all of them for a total profit of $700 in one season.

After our winter in Florida, we decided to head up north again to spend part of the summer in 1975. When we arrived at Sandy and Mark's farm, we were surprised to find that they had created a campsite for us on a field with a beautiful view overlooking the countryside. It was even complete with a flagpole and flag to mark our spot.

That summer we took each of our four grandchildren on separate vacations in the camper. Each child decided on their own where they wanted to go. John chose a trip to Cooperstown, New York, to visit the Baseball Hall of Fame. We stayed at a park where he and his grandpa went boating and fishing in a small pond. To this day, one of John's fondest memories of that trip was walking through the Hall of Fame with his grandfather and stopping at the plaque of Lou Gehrig. Bill explained to his young grandson all about the accomplishments Lou Gehrig made during his career. He told John that many of the records they saw that day would be broken during his lifetime but Gehrig's record of playing in 2,130 consecutive games would stand forever. Of course, neither one of them had any idea that a young man named Cal Ripken, Jr. was still attending high school and would not break into the major leagues for several more years. John wrote to his grandfather in 1995 when Cal Ripken, Jr. broke that record, recounting that day almost 20 years prior.

Dan was just out of first grade and he wanted to see dinosaurs, so we camped outside of Philadelphia and took him to museums. They had a children's museum he also enjoyed because it was full of interactive experiments. Eric, who was barely 4 years old at the time, chose a week at Lake Wallenpaupak, where he wanted to fish. This is a very large lake situated near the Pocono Mountains in Pennsylvania. Eric became fascinated with all of the chipmunk holes. He spent all of his time plugging up one hole, only to have a chipmunk come out of another hole. This went on all week, but it made him happy.

Julie was very young and was leery about leaving home so we took both her and her brother to a park close to home. She liked living in the camper; to her, it was a big doll house. They had a nice pool at the park, so we spent most of the time swimming.

When the summer was over, we headed back on the road for a slow trip back to Florida. We decided to make the trip more interesting by stopping at Civil War sites along the way. Since we were already in Pennsylvania, our first stop was in Gettysburg. The bus tour was incredibly sad but unforgettable. The sound track on the tour included the sounds of young boys groaning and dying on the battlefield. What was so surprising was how small the fields were where the actual battles took place. The soldiers could easily look each other in the eye from that short of a distance.

After Gettysburg we traveled to Fredericksburg, Virginia, where a battle occurred in December of 1862, and then on to Chancellorsville, about 20 miles away, where a battle took place in 1863. After that we visited the Wilderness, where the Civil War was fought in 1864. We also stopped by Petersburg, Virginia, and finally onto Appomattox, where the Civil War ended on April 9, 1865.

We stopped at many of the battlefields throughout the South and we could not fathom how difficult it must have been to have a war without modern day communication. By the time any messages or reconnaissance was received, the situation might have been entirely different. After our trip though Virginia we also stopped in Tennessee to see the battlefields in Murfreesboro and Chickamauga, which covered an area of about 130 miles. The campaign in Vicksburg, Mississippi, was fascinating because it seemed to us that the South had an excellent chance of blockading the North and cutting off their supply lines.

We also stopped in Georgia at the Missionary Ridge battle and at one of most shocking areas of our visit, the Andersonville prison in Georgia. I never expected it to be so small. At the height of the war, 33,000 men were imprisoned on a 26-acre site.

When we arrived in Florida, Daytona Beach looked like a perfect place for us to park because we were allowed to drive our car or motorcycle on the beach. We could also park the camper on the beach close to the boardwalk. It was incredible to lie in bed at night listening to the ocean waves rolling onto the shore. We stayed there about a month, and during that short time, a few problems crept into our paradise. The salt air and the ocean spray really did a job on us. Our bottle gas regulator on the trailer stopped working so we could not use the gas stove. Also, our toaster, vacuum, and anything with exposed electrical parts started to erode. We never expected this to happen in such a short time. Of course we were awfully close to the water and we had our doors and windows wide open because we had no air conditioning in the camper. Neither Bill nor I cared for the air-conditioning so we would just open up the doors and let the breeze come in. I learned why people living by the beach have so much money; they need to in order to replace their appliances every couple of years.

Our next stop was the Twin Lakes Park in Orlando. By this time, we realized our little motorcycle was getting too uncomfortable to ride for any length of time so we decided to look for a larger bike. Even though we were looking at used motorcycles, we still needed some extra money because our current one was not worth much as a trade-in. Since we were in the heart of orange country, we decided to get jobs as pickers in one of the groves. I must admit we were lousy pickers. To pick oranges we needed to carry a heavy burlap sack over our shoulder. We filled the bags and then dumped them into a large bin about the size of two bathtubs. It took us about 15 minutes to fill up a bag, and about two-and-a-half hours working together to fill a single bin. We were paid $6 for each tub we filled, so we made a combined total of about $18 a day. Although we were not making a lot of money, I looked at it as ideal because I could be with Bill all day long, which meant that I was alright and I could also keep an eye on my husband's diabetes. Besides, $18 a day was more than enough gas money for a few days of traveling.

To add to all of the fun of carrying around the bag for the oranges, we also had to move a heavy wooden ladder all around the tree to get to the high fruit. I could not go up the ladder, so Bill climbed up and threw the oranges to me or on the ground, and I put them in the tub. The local migrant workers who worked the fields got a kick out of watching us work. Often they would help us at the end of the day. Bill and I could never fill more than three tubs a day, and quite often the other workers would help us fill up the third tub if it did not look like we were going to make it. The oranges were mainly harvested in early spring, and once in a while if a frost was coming, the farmers brought out large smudge pots that they lit to keep the fruit from freezing at night.

After we had honed our picking skills in the orange groves, we also tried our hands at other crops. First we tried the tomato fields, but the rows were so low to the ground that the work killed our backs. Strawberry picking, however, was much different. The farmers hilled the fields so we were actually walking below the plants. Each picker was given a row. Instead of stopping to pick the berries, we would keep a slow walk and only pick the really ripe berries that we spotted on the plants. We would leave the baskets in the walk space until we had filled eight baskets, then we would put them in a flat and take them to the truck waiting in the field. On average we filled a basket in seven minutes, so by the end of the day we each filled 10 flats. We made $1 per flat, so at the end of the day we made $20 combined.

Similar to today, the majority of the workers were from Mexico or Central America. Most of the workers had their families out in the fields with them. The youngest children would gather the baskets and put them in a flat. Bill usually put our baskets together so I would not have to walk as far. When we all completed a row, we would hop into the truck and ride to the next field to start over again. The next day we started in the first spot again and picked from the beginning, thereby always picking nice ripe berries. The berries from these fields were flown to fine restaurants around the country. Unlike our counterparts, we constantly snacked on the strawberries while we worked. I guess they would want them all to go into the baskets, but we looked at it as if we were making $20 a day in labor plus another dollar or two in strawberries as a bonus.

One of my most memorable moments in our travels happened one day in these strawberry fields. Bill was working a few rows ahead of me when he yelled, "Hey honey, catch. It's a present from me to you." Bill had found a strawberry that was about four times the size of a normal berry and was ironically shaped like a heart. It was one of the many thoughtful gifts I received over the years and nothing ever tasted sweeter.

With the money we saved we were able to buy a used 500-horsepower Harley Davidson for a few hundred dollars. Bill put a lot of work into it and we always had difficulty finding the parts we needed because it was so old, but this bike was a lot more comfortable and much faster. We rode all over Florida on it, visiting places such as Cypress Gardens, Sea World, and the Historic Bok Sanctuary near Orlando. The Bok Sanctuary was an unforgettable experience that people should see. It is a sanctuary with beautiful gardens, birds, and a carillon that plays every 15 minutes. It is one of the quietest and most serene places we ever visited. We felt like we should be whispering the entire time. We left the area feeling very peaceful and tranquil. At the time we went they did not even charge an admission to get inside.

Part of the fun of riding our motorcycle around each state was seeing the reactions on people's faces when we stopped. On one of our rides we stopped at a fruit and vegetable stand and loaded up our little carrier on the cycle, but we still had quite a bit more for me to carry. The owner of the stand got a kick out of watching how much I could balance at one time so he decided to bring over a flat of two dozen eggs set in the cups of an open cardboard tray and told me they were free if I could carry them. I told him to hold on to them for just a minute while I juggled the items I had, then said, "Okay, now lay them on top." He had visions of us being splattered with raw eggs as soon as we started up. Luckily, I had learned that if I relaxed on the cycle there was no need to hold on. My body would go along as if I was part of the motorcycle. The owner lost his bet, and we made it home without a single broken egg. I always loved fun challenges.

The following summer of 1976 we found ourselves back at our campsite on Mark and Sandy's farm. We used this as a base camp and decided to visit my brother Bill who had been living in Cape Cod for quite some time. He ran a charter fishing boat for tourists in the area. We took a ride out to his place and stopped in Mystic, Connecticut, along the way. Mystic has wonderful sea museums in addition to Navy ships which we toured. I loved touring the ships and found all of them to be very interesting. However, I did have quite a bit of difficulty on the tour of a submarine. Just the thought of it scared me to death but I convinced myself I would at least have to try. Before we even started out on our travels, I told myself that I could not allow myself to miss out on any of the adventures this country had to offer and that at times I was going to have to suck it up and persevere. There was a long line of people waiting to get into the submarine. Finally we were in and oh my, never did I visualize it being so small and cramped inside. I got about a quarter of the way through when the sweat started pouring out of me. Bill was holding my hand and giving me support. Finally I told to him I could not do it and turned around to head out. Unfortunately, this was a one-way tour, and the area we were in was really only wide enough for one person, but I was so desperate that I quickly made it room enough for two. One person was going the wrong way – me. I am sure I was not the first person that left in the wrong direction, but it was still embarrassing.

When we arrived at my brother's place, he took us co-hogging which was a lot of fun. We stood in water up to our hips with rakes. The objective was to rake as deep as possible until we felt what might be a rock. I hit one, hooked it onto the rake, and pulled it up. I now had a very large clam. We got a bunch of them and had a fresh clam chowder for supper. I thought it was delicious. My Bill, who hates fish, just ate in silence.

P-town, or Providence, the last town on the Cape out on the point, is a wonderful place to visit. On Saturday afternoons all of the shops have different crafts to sell. These were not the ordinary crafts we saw in most tourist shops. I had never seen such beautiful work with glass stone, wood, or metal. It was very expensive but exquisite work. After sunset, we noticed that the atmosphere seemed to be changing. It seems that in P-town, the law says that as long as they restrict themselves to just Saturday night, they can do what they do. I stood there open-mouthed. The whole town opened up to the gay community. (This was not widely published in the 1970s.) Out of everywhere came people dressed in their finery. There were beautiful gowns, feather boas, fancy tuxedos, leather and chains, and the works. A car could not even drive down the road; it was like Times Square on New Year's Eve. I was having the time of my life taking it all in, but a couple of guys tried to hit on Bill and he didn't appreciate that. I guess they liked his beard. I told Bill not to complain because we were the intruders.

We stayed in Cape Cod for 10 days and then headed off to see the Blue Ridge Mountains through Virginia and North Carolina. The scenery was beautiful during the day, but at sunset it started to get foggy. The higher we drove into the mountains, the foggier it got, until we were blanketed in a pea soup fog. We crept along slowly until we finally found a campground, turned in, and parked in a spot for the night. We had never been in fog this bad. When we woke in the morning the sun was shining and we went outside to look around. What we saw was that our camper wheels were on plenty of solid ground, and the camper was hooked to the truck, but the back of the camper was actually hanging over the mountain's edge which we found out was at an elevation of 3,740 feet. There was a low wall around the edge, so in the fog I guess Bill stopped when he hit it and pulled up a little. I don't think I would have slept well knowing our bedroom was hanging over the side of a mountain for the night. Besides our evening hanging over a mountain, the rest of our ride back to Florida was fairly uneventful. We decided to stay at the Twin Lakes Campground again because it was close to Walt Disney World, which we had not yet seen. The Disney World was a lot of fun, even without young children running around. At the time, it was the amusement park only; they had just started to build what would become Epcot Center.

It was now towards the end of 1976 and we were getting ready to head out to see the rest of our country. However, on one of our motorcycle rides, we ran into our first problem. The truck drivers respected people on motorcycles, but the bus drivers did not. We had a Greyhound bus driver actually edge us off the highway onto the grass with a big grin on his face. We did not have enough power to beat him, and we could have been seriously injured from his nasty little prank. When we returned to the park, we came to the realization that since our intention was to use the motorcycle extensively whenever we were parked at a campground, we could not expose ourselves to a situation like that again.

To solve this problem, we once again needed to purchase a larger motorcycle. To accomplish this, we also needed to go back to work for a short time. We found a job where we could work together at a Ramada Inn near Orlando working nights in the laundry. We sorted out all the laundry so it was all set for the day workers. We did this for a couple of months so we could trade the Harley in for the biggest motorcycle we could afford. We purchased a Yamaha 1100. Just like cars, the 1977 models were out for around $3,000 but we found a brand new 1976 that a dealer was trying to sell to make room for the new models. We were able to purchase it for $1,700. Bill and I only made minimum wage at the hotel, but we worked six days a week and soon enough we had the bike paid for. This motorcycle was very good to us. We actually ended up keeping this same bike until we were 65 years old. This bike had such power that with just a little twist of the wrist we could leave anyone in the dust. We never had a bad incident after that.

Actually, we never had an accident on the motorcycle, but we kept getting pulled over by the police quite often in all different states. It was not for speeding. I thought it would be funny to glue a long black wig to my helmet. It looked hilarious. Truckers would laugh their heads off as we passed by, then get on their CB radios and tell the next trucker to watch for us. I had a great time riding behind Bill, waving to the people tooting at us. The police unfortunately were not as amused. It was always the same routine. First the flashing lights to pull us over, then the policeman would walk up to us ready to give me a ticket for not wearing a helmet. When they realized I covered the helmet with a wig they did not appreciate it. In all of our travels around the country, I can honestly say we never once came across a cop with a sense of humor for my idea. Nevertheless, I still kept the wig on the helmet for six years.

Since we were using the motorcycle for longer and longer distances, we also purchased a trailer that could be towed by the cycle. It was 4 feet by 4 feet with a double flat top. The trailer unfolded from the top and turned into a 4-foot by 8-foot platform. We stuck poles into the side brackets and slipped a tent over the poles and this is where we slept. Underneath the platform was storage for our sleeping bags, camping stove, lamp, clothes, cooking supplies, and dishes. We would go out this way for as little as a month and as long as six months. People were always fascinated when we set up for the night on our cycle trips. We had it down to such a routine we could be all set up in less than 10 minutes. When we were back at our regular camper for a long move, the trailer fit snugly inside the camper. We tried to use the motorcycle whenever possible, even on short stops, because it was so much cheaper than driving the pickup, which only got seven to 10 miles per gallon.

Our intentions were to head out to Texas in August but we met a woman in Florida who worked a carnival every year and talked us into trying it. Although we never considered this before, Bill and I thought we would give it a try. So in August we decided to try our hands at the carnival life. The carnival worked around towns in Pennsylvania, New York, and Ohio. We first dropped our bike off at the farm and headed for Meadville, Pennsylvania, to join the carnival. To say the least, it was quite an experience. The "carnies" are literally a race of their own. The carnival is their whole world. As far as we could tell, nothing else existed for them. For one thing, the carnies stick together like mud and will gang up on anyone that dares to try to do anything to any one of them. Bill always felt that I was very well protected, and I was.

The game we worked was the basketball toss. Yes, some games are almost impossible to win, but most are not. The principle is to give the winner a tiny little prize. If they are lucky enough to win again, they can trade up for a bigger prize. The carnies' job is to keep talking the customer into trading up for a bigger prize, thereby getting them to spend more and more money. Bill and I got really good at it, and by the end of the season on the first of October we had made $2,000. We immediately used the money to pick up our motorcycle and pay a welder to put a rack on the back to hold the bike. This made it much easier to load and unload the bike. The rest of the money was a little nest egg to use for the following year of traveling.

In 10 years we covered a large portion of the country. We visited every state on the mainland. Since Bill saw Hawaii during the war, and I was not going to fly on an airplane or take a boat for that length of time, it was not on our list. We always traveled north to south, parking our trailer for at least a month in one spot. We would get to know the locals; they were always the ones who could tell us some of the good places to go to that only they knew about. We have such a beautiful country. This part of our life, our travels, is not meant to be a travelogue. I want to tell more about the different experiences Bill and I had while we traveled. We did visit all of the major museums in the country as well as ballparks, hall of fames, national parks, and caverns. We stopped at zoos, historical sites, aquariums, waterfalls, ski resorts, beaches, colleges, wineries, and factory tours. We learned all about glass making, candy making, Indian pottery, and basket weaving. We saw it all. I should have kept a log as we traveled, but it did not occur to me at the time.

My stories may not be in the correct order that they occurred, but I do remember all of our travels. The best part of our trips was being together and spending time as a couple. Many of the memories that stand out were from some of our simplest moments. For instance, we ate a picnic lunch on the lawn of every capitol we could, and were never thrown off. Of course that excludes Washington D.C. The fence was too hard to climb.

After leaving Florida and the carnival life, we decided to head west. Our first stop was in Huntsville, Alabama. We stopped at the U.S. Space and Rocket Center where we lucked out. They were giving a tour to schoolchildren, and Bill and I just latched onto the tour. They explained everything in simple language so the children as well as Bill and I understood it. The best part was hearing about all of the gene experiments they were working on. The guide explained that they could grow a mouse with whatever kind of tail they wanted it to have. It could be straight or curly, long or short, or none at all. He showed us all the different mice and how they accomplished each difference. The children and we were fascinated.

As we rode to Tennessee we hit a very bumpy road but thought nothing of it. Much to our surprise, when we stopped at a campground and went into our camper, we found that the whole floor had buckled up by a half foot. It seemed the weight of our motorcycle was too much for the back of the camper. Also, our new tires were wearing crooked. Bill worked on the inside of the camper and got it back to normal. Our next problem was how to transport our cycle. With a fifth wheel the camper is hooked up inside the truck bed so we could not store much of anything except for a couple of lawn chairs. Our solution was to get rid of the fifth wheel camper and get a regular trailer we could pull with a truck hitch. With the truck bed empty, we could carry the motorcycle as well as the cycle trailer. We went to a camper dealer to see what kind of a deal we could make. The owner wanted a fifth wheeler for himself so we did an even trade, our 35-foot fifth wheeler for a 28-foot trailing camper. Both parties were satisfied. Bill spent another two weeks building a cap for the back of the truck so it would be fully enclosed and locked. It was tall enough that we could stand up in the back and it was large enough to hold the motorcycle, spare parts, the cycle trailer, and some lawn chairs.

After our little delay, we were set to tour the Tennessee River. The main feature we wanted to see was the lock system along the river. The man working at one of the locks was really very friendly and asked if we would like to explore a lock. The personal tour was fine as he explained everything that was above ground. But then he said, "Follow me, and I'll take you down to the dynamos." Oh my Lord, he took us to a metal hole about 3 feet around with a long set of metal ladder steps that I believed just might reach hell. I looked down that hole and said, "No way." The man, probably an engineer, said, "I'll go first, you next, then your husband, and we will surround you and you'll be okay." This was one of those days where I had to squelch my fear or the experience would be lost. Down, down, down, we went. I will admit with the men surrounding me I did pretty well by my standards. I wonder now if they were scared at all. The noise was loud at the bottom by the dynamos. He told us about how the equipment operated and the unbelievable amount of pressure that was pushing on the cement wall behind us. I pointed out to him that water was leaking in through a crack in the wall. My concern was the wall might be cracking apart while we were way down there under the river. He responded, "No problem, we have pumps working all the time so the water you are standing in doesn't get more than six inches deep." My next question was "Can we go back up now?" We returned to the surface, said our goodbyes and he complimented me on being a good sport. I think we had to run home so I could change my underpants.

Continuing through Tennessee, I wanted to try to see the Delta Queen on the Mississippi River in Memphis. We got to look at it, but we decided not to spend the money to take a ride, although that would have been fun. Instead we stopped by one of the more famous hotels in the South, the Peabody Hotel in Memphis. The Peabody had a large water fountain in the lobby with a little pool at the base. The fountain must have been a good 12 feet high, and the pond covered at least a similar diameter. The manager did not say why, but he told us to come back to the lobby around 10 a.m. The next day, we were standing outside the hotel when someone stopped traffic and a parade of ducks crossed the street, walked into the hotel, and hopped into the pool. At that moment, we did not realize this was a tradition at The Peabody, we just thought it was nice of the hotel to allow the ducks to visit despite the mess they were going to make.

After our trip to Memphis, we stopped in Kentucky to see some horses and try a mint julep or two. We passed the famous Claiborne Farm with a sign posted outside that read "Home of Secretariat." There was only one beautiful horse in the pasture so we hoped we actually saw the horse. We stopped by another farm that provided tours of the grounds. The tour guide was elegantly dressed, and the place was immaculate. Each horse had its own stable boy and the guide gave us the history of each horse. We did not know enough about horses to appreciate their family tree, but we knew we were looking at winners.

I must confess I did not behave myself at Churchill Downs. It was nice because in the 1970s it was quite common that we could walk into many of these famous places such as racetracks or baseball stadiums free of charge if an event was not going on. It is quite different today with everything under lock and key. I decided to horse around, so I was prancing off the track to the winner's circle to get my wreath of roses when I collapsed into a heap on the ground. I had stepped into a large hole and badly sprained my ankle. I could not understand how a hole could be there. If a horse stepped in it, it could have easily broken a leg. As Bill helped me limp off the track to our cycle he gave me a small lecture on always horsing around, but I was only pretending to listen.

By the time we got back to our trailer my ankle swelled up so much that Bill had to cut the boot off of my foot. I was none too happy about losing a pair of boots I liked, but I cannot honestly say I learned my lesson either.

After our trip through Kentucky, we continued to head north up through Indiana. Our highlight of this state was a tour of the Indianapolis Motor Speedway, home of the Indianapolis 500. I was forced to behave myself here because they would not let us race around the track on our motorcycle. Instead, the tour took place on a shuttle bus that took us around the track. I am sure we could have done it much faster and enjoyed it more. After the track, we toured the museum connected to the speedway. This held Bill's interest for quite some time since all men love their cars.

Our next stop was a brief one in Michigan again to visit Mackinaw and Mackinac Island. The only way to get there was by ferryboat, and when we arrived we rented a small bicycle for transportation. We rode around the whole island on our bike, which was a nice, peaceful ride. When we returned the bike, we hopped back on the Yamaha to drive across a very long bridge from Mackinaw to St. Ignas. Lake Michigan is on one side of the bridge and Lake Huron is on the other. It was a really high bridge over the water, and the wind howled throughout the area. At times when the wind was too strong, the bridge actually closed. We rode across it on our cycle. It was a little tricky because the road on the bridge was actually made of metal grating. It was not very easy to control our bike on the grates.

On the way back it started to rain hard and the wind came up like we could not believe. I was sure they would not let anyone on the bridge at that point, but those of us on it had to keep going to get off. Bill yelled to me to sit as close to him as possible and not let the wind get between us. We slipped and slid all over the place and gusts of wind actually had us airborne at times. I really and truly felt that we were going to wind up in the lake far below us. I thought to myself that if we have to go, at least we would go together. We made it, but that was one of the scariest moments we ever faced on our motorcycle.

Another one of our close calls took place during what started as a leisurely ride through Texas. We stopped in Texarkana, which is, naturally, on the Texas-Arkansas border. We saw a sign that read "Boats for rent. Explore the bayou." That sounded like a good time, so the next day we headed for our boat ride. The boat was what they call a flat bottom. It had about a 10-foot flat bottom and was square across both ends. The way to move the boat was to stand up and push a long pole into the ground to push the boat forward. The bayou was very eerie. We could barely even see the water because it was filled solid with lily pads. Amazingly the water was probably only 2 feet deep. To add to the feeling, cypress trees grew out of the water everywhere. All the trees were full of hanging moss and very different looking – sort of like a Hitchcock movie.

Before we headed out into the bayou, the clerk asked us how long we intended to stay out on our tour. We told him about an hour. The clerk replied, "Okay, if you are not back in an hour and a half, we will come out looking for you." When we got out to the creek entrance and into the bayou we understood his statement. It all looked the same. We realized how easily anyone could get lost in this area. I left it up to Bill to get us back.

We were pushing our poles along nicely. Bill was in the back and I was up front when Bill noticed we were taking on water. I was so interested in the scenery, looking for birds and other wildlife that I did not notice I was standing in water. All of a sudden the water was coming in fast. The sides of the boat were very low so naturally it would not take too much to swamp the boat. I was yelling at Bill to do something since I was petrified we were going to sink. Bill quickly looked at the bottom of the boat and realized the water was coming in from the front. He hurried up front where he could now see the water bubbling into the boat. Bill put his hand over it and felt a hole. That is when he figured out that I had kicked the drain plug out of the boat. I can only imagine I must have done it while I was busy looking at the scenery. Quite frankly, I did not know there was a plug in the bottom of the boat. I searched around and found the plug while Bill had his hand pressed against the hole and he got the plug screwed back into place. We bailed out as much water as possible with our hands so we could push the boat back to the dock with our poles. When we finally got back we told the man about what happened and how worried we were that the alligators would get us. He kind of chuckled and said, "Don't worry, the snakes would have gotten you first." Bill and I just looked at each other and said nothing. I started to wonder if we going to survive our travels.

Next we headed for Brownsville, Texas, which is near South Padre Island and the Mexican border. We stopped at the King Ranch, which at 825,000 acres is the largest ranch in the country. The ranch is actually larger than the state of Rhode Island. We could ride and ride all day and still be on King Ranch land. We stayed at a campground in Brownsville for several months and the owners really made an effort to ensure that we enjoyed their place. One day they even rented an elephant so that we could all go on elephant rides. Another time they got a truck full of watermelons and we had a watermelon festival. The campground had over a hundred campers, most of them snowbirds that enjoyed the cheap seasonal rates in Texas.

We used the campsite in Texas to cross over the Mexican border to visit Matamoras. This place offered a truly different culture and experience for Bill and me. When we entered the country, there were kids doing handstands, somersaults, or anything they could do to beg for money. The trouble was that a group of bigger kids was standing off in the distance, ready to take away any money they made as soon as we walked away. The area was a field of shacks next to the Rio Grande, mostly made of tin, cardboard, or anything that people could find. As far as we could tell, none of the homes had plumbing and I only saw one outhouse in the place. These poor people walked ankle-deep in muck, which could have very well been sewage. I could not understand how these children could even survive. When we wanted to buy any of the wares they were peddling on the streets, such as belts, purses, wallets, and blouses, we were expected to barter for it. I must confess, we were not very good at this. How could we even think about trying to get a better deal for something when we saw firsthand how these people lived?

At the campground we were warned to watch ourselves closely when in Mexico. Many of the police worked on a bribery system and took advantage of the tourists. If they could find any reason at all to stop a person, they would. If stopped by the police, tourists were forced many times to pay a substantial bribe before they would be let go. After that, we stayed out of Matamoras.

When we returned to the United States, we followed the Rio Grande until we arrived at Big Bend National Park. Although this park is not well known outside of Texas, it was worth the trip. This park was actually almost as large as the King Ranch (800,000 acres). It started at the Rio Grande and continued up through the Chisos Mountains. Mexicans would come across the river on burros and sell trays full of fancy stones for a dollar. At night we could hear the coyotes yipping away. Campers in the area were warned not to leave their puppies tied outside at night or any time they were away from the trailer because they would be taken away by wild animals. Apparently the coyotes liked puppy meals.

We would sit and watch the Mexicans cut rush in the river, bundle it up, and float it to the little village nearby. They used it for the roofs on their small adobe homes. From what we could see, it was a much greener and cleaner existence than that of the people closer to the major towns.

When we arrived in El Paso we found out President Ford was coming to town to give a speech at the University of Texas-El Paso. We watched amongst a large crowd as Air Force One pulled into the airport. Bill and I were right next to the road as the president's limo drew near. I was waving as Bill reached in his pocket for a handkerchief. In two seconds, Bill was flat on the ground with security men on top of him. I have to give security an A-plus for their reaction time, but by the same token my Bill gets an F-minus for not thinking. Take a lesson from this. If you are EVER near the president, stand still and do not make any sudden movements, especially into your pocket.

Just outside of El Paso is a beautiful area called the Hueco Tanks. The place gets its name from the soft red rock outcroppings surrounding the area that have many large holes in them. Some of the holes were up to 6 feet deep and about 10 feet across. Back in the time of the California Gold Rush, the 49'ers heading west used this area as a watering stop. There were also many shallow caves where travelers wrote their names along with the year of their trip and any new birth or death announcements. The park rangers did a wonderful job of keeping close guard of Hueco Tanks, so this bit of history was preserved.

After we left El Paso, we decided to stay for a short time on a Cherokee Indian Reservation near Jacksonville, Texas. I had hopes of learning how the Native Americans made pottery and wove baskets but it did not happen. We left after a month because we never felt comfortable in the area. To be blunt, the people tolerated the "white man" visiting their area solely for the tourist dollars, but they were not going to help us. I cannot blame them in the least. What we as a country did to the American Indians is unthinkable. Unfortunately, from what we saw out West, in many areas we are still doing the same thing to the Native Americans.

After seeing all we could in Texas, we headed northeast and arrived in Oklahoma. Of all the hall of fames and museums we visited, I would have to say my favorite was the National Cowboy and Western Heritage Museum in Oklahoma City, Oklahoma. This museum was a large compound consisting of several buildings covering every aspect of cowboy life, from ranch activities to the poems they wrote while out on the range. Bill was always a sports fan so I am sure his favorites were either the Baseball Hall of Fame in New York or the Football Hall of Fame in Ohio, but for anyone interested in learning more about the West, this museum is a great place to start.

Following Oklahoma, we made our way on our motorcycle to Omaha, Nebraska. The Midwest states were flat, and we rode for hours just looking at corn. Suddenly, Mother Nature wanted to make it more exciting for us so she sent a tornado. It was off in the distance, but those suckers are fast. Bill was having the time of his life. Usually when we rode and I thought he was driving too fast I would give him a poke in the ribs with my thumbs. I am sure he was thinking, "Mamma won't poke me today." We outran the tornado but it was scary. If we had misjudged the speed, we literally had no place to go if it got too close. I could not imagine lying down in a ditch or hiding in an underpass with a tornado roaring past. The only safe place for me was a long ways from the tornado.

The reason for our trip to Omaha was to see Boy's Town. Boy's Town was a place open to any troubled, abused, or unwanted child. This was a place to be proud of. Anyone who entered the gate was welcome and given clean clothes and wholesome food. The children were provided a home atmosphere but at the same time were taught manners and required to attend church services. Boy's Town was pretty much self-sufficient. They raised animals for food, grew crops, and learned trades such as shoe making and tailoring. Each boy had to take his turn at being a guide. They were so polite, mannerly, and respectful; I just can't praise them enough! Every occupation was available for them to learn. There was a dairy barn, vegetable farm, bakery, barbershop, auto repair shop; you name it, they had it. They lived in separate houses, each with four to six boys and a set of parents. We looked at each other thinking the same thing – this could be our calling. We found out, however, that people signed up years in advance, and we were not ready to settle down again. At the end of the tour, the area had a sign thanking us for our interest in Boy's Town and that any donations were appreciated. I must say that everyone around us on the tour, including Bill and I, dug deep into our pockets that day.

Some of our other summer travels included a trip through the Dakotas, which was simply no man's land. We rode all day on our cycle and never saw a soul. All along the road there were mounds of rock in the fields shaped like 3-foot high pyramids. They were not land markers because some were too close. Bill's explanation was that the pyramids were for the shepherds to sit and lean against when sheep graze in the area. We never did find out the answer.

One of the main reasons to travel through the Dakotas was to see Mt. Rushmore up close. Unfortunately, we found out that tourists are kept quite a distance away from the monument. I would have preferred to get much closer. On the next mountain over was a monument in the process of being built to honor Crazy Horse. One generation started the project and now the next generation had taken over. As of today, it will still require the efforts of future generations to finish it. The scale of the project was incredible. When we were there around 1980, a bulldozer was working in the eye of the horse. There were telescopes available so tourists could watch them work, and there was a museum that displayed the project. The family working on this project was very close to the Dakota Indian tribes. The curator of the museum was given objects by the local tribes that I had never seen anywhere else. The family was very proud of the museum and one of them was always there to explain things to tourists. The path to the museum was lined with busts of each of the different Indian chiefs. A few years later we read that someone snuck in and broke the noses off of every bust. This caused the family to consider closing the museum to the public.

On our way to our friends ranch in Montana our guardian angel was watching over us again. We asked at a campsite in Wyoming where we could find the closest place to eat breakfast. We wanted to put on a lot of miles that day so we decided to eat breakfast out. Since we were told the diner was only down the road apiece, Bill took his insulin before we left. I was leery of this because he needed to eat very quickly after taking the injection. We rode and rode and found no place to eat anywhere. Then I noticed he kept his hands on the handlebars but was pulling his arms outward. I knew we were running into trouble on the main highway. All I kept thinking was, "Please restaurant be around the next bend." Finally we saw a diner and I kept yelling at Bill "Pull in, I'm hungry!" If he were not to far into insulin shock he would listen to me but if he continued to lapse deeper into shock he ran the risk of going into a seizure and we would crash. Luckily he listened to me and pulled into the diner. I jumped off the bike and Bill sat there in a daze. I ran into the diner and grabbed a sugar bun out of the display case and ran back outside without paying. I pushed the bun into Bill's mouth and slowly he returned back to normal. We stayed and ate breakfast, and I paid for the sugar bun that I guess they thought I swiped. While eating I asked Bill why he was pulling his arms out while driving. He said, "I thought at the time that was how I made the motorcycle go." That was a close call but we continued to Montana and a new adventure.

Some friends of ours, the Cooley's, had a small ranch in Hamilton, Montana. We parked our trailer on their ranch so we could tour through Montana and Canada. Before we headed out, we enjoyed some time fishing with them. This is where I caught my first trout. Two weeks later we broke out the motorcycle and trailer and took off for a trip through Canada.

We started the trip by visiting Glacier National Park near the Canadian border. I wanted to hike through the mountains, but the "Caution: Bears" signs all over made us kind of skeptical. After the park, we traveled up into Calgary and then headed west to Vancouver. We traveled about 900 miles with side trips along the way to Banff, Lake Louise, and a beautiful unnamed waterfall up one of the northern routes. We were heading all the way to Vancouver, so we had many overnight stops. It was so nice in the evening. Everyone had campfires going, and the woods were dotted with them. We didn't have any bear problems, thank heavens. The parks had outside water pumps and outhouses. When necessary, if showers were not available, we would take a basin of water into our 4-foot-high tent and attempt to take a teacup bath. In Canada we opted instead to take baths in remote creeks in the frigid water. Bill would wash my hair for me and enjoyed rinsing it with pans of this icy water.

Bill was sold on Canada because the Queens Way, which runs clear across Canada from New Brunswick to Vancouver, had no speed limit. Bill was always curious to see what our cycle could do, so on this road he found out. I poked his ribs when the motorcycle reached 125 mph, and at one point I believe we were actually flying low. He was satisfied and got it out of his system.

The state parks in Canada are really nice. Each site is by itself, and at the entrance the rangers placed a pile of logs for the campers to use for campfires. They also provided a brochure on bear protection. One of the rules was that food needed to be hung from trees, not left on the ground. In addition, nothing with any scent was allowed inside of your sleeping area, not even deodorant or toothpaste. We decided to follow the rules very closely because here we were, in our little pop-up motorcycle tent, and one swipe from a bear would destroy it.

We took a long boat ride to Vancouver Island and rode the length of the island on the motorcycle. When we pulled into Victoria it seemed like Christmas; there were white lights everywhere. The municipal building was like a mansion, with lights outlining the entire building and every single window. It was like that all the time. I was very surprised to find a Chinatown in Victoria; we had some great Chinese suppers. We also found a museum dedicated to totem poles. The guides explained which tribes were represented and the meaning of each totem pole. This was one of the most unique museums we toured.

We headed back to the ranch to get out of this border area before the first snow of the season fell in the pass. On our way back, we stopped by Little Bighorn to see the area of Custer's Last Stand. We were very surprised to see how small of an area the battle actually encompassed. It was much different than what we had seen in the movies. The battle was south of Billings, and we saw monuments regarding the battle in several places in Montana and even into Wyoming.

An American Love Story

Montana summers are very short, possibly two months. I know it is cliché to mention Big Sky Country in Montana, but unless you have seen it for yourself, you just cannot grasp the size and scope. We never saw a more beautiful sky in our lifetime. The amount of sky we saw at night was incredible. It felt like there were millions of stars we could reach out and touch.

After we left our friend's ranch, we continued south and headed down to Colorado to ride the trail ridge road over the Rocky Mountains. Our truck was very good to us through the mountains. It was loaded with our big motorcycle and trailer and was pulling our camper. Luckily, we made it over every mountain without a problem.

I believe Idaho Springs, Colorado, is the friendliest town in the United States. The houses all look neat and well maintained, and many have gingerbread work on the outside. We could not walk down the street without being invited on a porch or two to talk for a spell. The locals told us about St. Mary's Glacier that was located near there but could only be reached by a strenuous hike. A sign at the bottom said to walk for five minutes and check your pulse, and if it does not return to normal in seven minutes, do not continue the hike. It was ridiculously steep, but we made it. Once on top it was well worth the climb. The glacier was behind the top of the mountain. We just sat for hours and watched the water trickle off the glacier down the mountain a ways and run into a lake. This water was as clear as drinking water and bright blue from the sky's reflection. It was the most beautiful spot that I remember from all of our travels and well worth the hike. However, the walk down was not any easier than the climb up the mountain. We had to balance ourselves and plant our feet in the ground to prevent from falling forward. By the end of the hike, our shins felt like they were on fire.

In contrast to our beautiful trip through St. Mary's Glacier, we took a cycle ride and wound up in a box canyon. We made our supper by the tent, and when night hit, we found ourselves in total blackness. It was blacker than black and not a soul was in sight. Bill jokingly told me not to be afraid because Indians do not attack until daylight. Unfortunately for me, of all the times for it to happen, Bill's sugar dropped while we were sleeping and he went into convulsions. I scrambled out of the tent to find sugar in this pitch-black canyon. I managed to get some sugar into Bill, and all I could do was sit there and wait for him to come out of it. I felt like I was the only person in the world: there was no sound, no light, just blackness. I survived the night. As the sunrise approached, Bill came to. I cried and Bill hugged me. Life was good again.

After that adventure, we spent some time panning for gold, which was a lot of fun. We panned in Idaho Springs and collected some gold dust which we kept in a vial. We found one creek that the locals told us to try. Bill went out into the creek ahead of me. He looked the part of an old time prospector. He was wearing old jeans, a flannel shirt, a full-faced beard, and a floppy old prospector's leather hat we found at a garage sale. Before I got into the creek, a car stopped and the passengers stood on the side of the road watching what they thought was an old prospector panning for gold. They asked me if he had been panning awhile. I said yes and that I had been watching him for a quite awhile and he seemed to be finding gold. Other cars stopped. I never did get into the creek. I was having too much fun letting the tourists go home thinking they saw a real prospector panning for gold, not my husband whose experience amounted to a couple of hours.

Cripple Creek, Colorado, is an old mining town about 90 miles from Colorado Springs, near Pikes Peak. There was an old, closed up turquoise mine on top of the hill. When it rained, turquoise would wash out of the dirt piled around the mine. We found small pieces of turquoise right along the hill. We found two stones that were actually large enough to have earrings made for me.

From there we traveled to Manitou Springs, Colorado, where we were told of another good hike. This hike was not as steep a climb as St. Mary's Glacier, but it wound clear around the mountain. On top of the mountain were blue birds the size of hawks. They were bright blue and dozens of them circled the area. Over the side of the other mountain we could see the Seven Falls area, where a beautiful waterfall dropped down the mountain in seven distinct steps. We marveled at this site while listening to the clarion echo every 15 minutes from the Will Rogers Memorial. We just laid back and enjoyed this spot. I am sure it is obvious that Colorado was our favorite state.

We took the tram up Pikes Peak. When we got above the tree line, the marmots came out to greet us. These animals were bigger than rabbits, and as soon as they heard the tram coming, they sat on the hill along the track to watch it go by.

Our travels through Colorado continued as we rode up Mt. Evans on our motorcycle. At 14,264 feet above sea level, it is the highest road in the United States. Although Mt. Rainier in Washington is actually higher at 14,410 feet, I guess the road over it does not reach the high spot. To add to the adventure, we were above the clouds on top of Mt. Evans, which was a first for me because I had never been in an airplane. Going up the mountain was fine, but coming down we realized there was no railing of any kind and we were very close to the edge.

One of our finest adventures took place just outside of Alamogordo, New Mexico, near Holloman Air Force Base. We first stopped and checked out the White Sands National Monument. The dunes are actually made out of gypsum, and they were so white the glare from the sun ruined the pictures. We explored the area for quite awhile then continued down U.S. Highway 70 towards Las Cruces. Little did we know this stretch of road also passed through the White Sands Missile Range and a sign had been erected behind us while we were in the White Sands area that said "Do Not Enter" because of a missile test taking place across the highway. We of course could not see the sign, so we headed on down the road. We were driving directly into a fierce headwind, barely going 10 miles an hour up the long hill. Halfway through our truck ran out of gas, which to us was no problem since we always kept an extra five-gallon gas can with us. We got out to put gas in our truck when all of a sudden a soldier appeared in a jeep. He was checking the road to make sure no one was on it. Much to his surprise, he found us on the side of the highway. He called the command center, and we heard them reply back, "Get them the hell out of there." We were rushed into the jeep and had no choice but to leave our camper, truck, cycle, and trailer behind. While we were riding in the back, the driver was telling the command center how close we were to the exit. Then, over the radio, we heard, "Countdown. Get out." The soldier floored the gas pedal on that jeep like never before while we were listening to the countdown on the radio. "10, 9, 8, 7…," and we were still driving like crazy. "6, 5, 4…," and we were at the exit. "3…," and we made it to the overlook. "2, 1…," and bingo, the missiles flew right over everything we owned. None of the missiles had any problems, and it all ended well. The soldier drove us back to our rig, and we went back to filling the gas tank. The soldier asked us how we could have missed the sign. We told him that there was no "Do Not Enter" sign when we entered White Sands, and that if there were one, we never would have missed it. It was just one of those instances; we were on the road seconds before the sign went up. I never fully understood how it happened, but it sure made for an exciting ride.

We continued our travels through New Mexico and visited many of the Indian reservations throughout the state. We started about 60 miles outside of Albuquerque where the Acoma tribe lived. There was only one trail up the mesa, which was a strategy that allowed them to easily protect themselves. They allowed tourists to make the trek but more or less ignored them, as this was their home site. These people still lived exactly like they did centuries ago. Their homes were still made of adobe and they cooked in outdoor clay ovens. The Acoma Indians are famous for the horsehair pottery that comes from this area.

Next we headed west of Las Cruces towards Demming, New Mexico, to the Gila Cliff Dwellings. Although the tribes were long gone, the rangers kept the ladders there so people could climb throughout the dwellings from one level to another. Each cave had a separate function. For example, one was for sleeping and another for grain storage. We walked along a narrow ledge to get from one cave to another. The people grew corn on the top of the cliffs, which were high off the ground and inaccessible to enemies. It was an ingenious setup.

While taking a ride in New Mexico, we came across a dirt road, and off in the distance we could see some old houses. We turned down the road and drove under a wooden arch that was beautifully decorated with flowers. On the arch was a sign that stated, "Enter Slowly, We Love Our Children." It was a neat little place that only had nine or 10 homes at the most. Most of the homes were well decorated with flowers, and although the people still looked like hippies from the 1960s, they seemed like one big, happy family. As we drove through, we saw children and adults playing together. We rode to the end of the street, turned around, and rode away without stopping. The children waved at us but we felt like we did not have any right to intrude on these people who had found a peaceful, loving life.

Continuing west and not too far over the Arizona-New Mexico border was a place called the Dragoon mountain range where we stopped at Cochise Stronghold Memorial Park. It was the spot on a desert rise where Cochise held up with his followers. There was just one narrow entrance, which made it very difficult for the army to get at him. There is nothing there anymore, but all of the trees and bushes are labeled as to their use. Some were medicines, others were sweets to eat or spices for cooking. Just about all of their needs were satisfied by what they could find in those trees and bushes. I often wondered how they went about learning what was poisonous and what was not. Perhaps if someone committed a crime, they had to eat a new berry or leaf or bark as their punishment to learn the effect.

After seeing New Mexico, we headed up through Arizona to the Grand Canyon. *Let's have a little "yeah" for the girls: A ranger told us that when girls hike from the south rim to the north rim of the Grand Canyon, they do it in better time than the boys.* Of course I am not sure if they are better hikers or if they are just more leery of being down there. We walked all along the rim of the canyon, but we did not take the long hike down to the bottom. It was much too warm when we arrived to dare to take that hike.

We decided to break character for a short time when we arrived in Phoenix. There was a beautiful campground that cost more for one single night than we normally paid for a week, but we wanted to see how the other half went camping in their snazzy motor homes and customized buses. Every site was surrounded with white stones and palm trees that were all lit up and quite elegant. The campground had three different temperature pools, so we tried each one. The bathhouse and showers were all tiled and mirrored. In the evening we headed for the recreation room to play pool. We walked in wearing our usual jeans and t-shirts and much to our surprise, we found a room full of men in suits and ties. As they gave us the look, we quickly turned around and marched out. I am sure they heard us laughing as we walked out, but we could not hold it in any longer.

We had a friend, Arlene, who lived in Tucson, Arizona, so we headed there next. She introduced us to her brother, who was a professor at the University of Arizona. He invited us to the university to tour his laboratory. I must say he was one of the most educated men I had ever met. He was working on the effects of different laser beams. The things he showed us were usually reserved for invited guests of the university. We were in awe of some of his breakthroughs and felt privileged to be there. When he was finished with his demonstration, he asked us if we had time to sit down and talk in his office. He said to us, "I showed you what I do, but I have heard about what you two have been doing for the past couple of years, so please tell me some stories." Needless to say, we were there for quite some time, and Bill and I could not believe how interested he was in our travels. To have a person who we considered to be a genius say, "You two are really great to know," sure was a nice ego boost.

One of the little towns we loved to visit was in between Phoenix and Flagstaff called Wickiup, Arizona. I like to say that name. Whenever we were close to it we stopped and fixed our lunch there. It consisted of a combined store, gas station, and problem solver for the six homes in Wickiup.

Each January, campers descended on the town Quartzite, Arizona, outside of Tucson for its annual jubilee. Normally Quartzite, which is about an hour east of Phoenix, is not much bigger than Wickiup. Since there was not much of a campground, campers would just park in the desert during the winter. Most of them were woodcarvers because the area contained ironwood, which is an extremely hard wood that is very popular with carvers. These were not run-of-the-mill wood carvers. Their work was sold worldwide. One carver was creating the chief of every Indian tribe for a museum. We stayed for a month, watching with interest how they went about carving these pieces. Bill was quite pleased with himself when he finished his carving of a pig. I was so proud of him because it actually looked pretty good. We went back to this same site in January for the stone carver's jubilee. People came from foreign countries to buy and sell. We never saw such creations from stone and wood as they we did there. I even had one of the local craftsmen make a pair of earrings for me from some of the turquoise we found in Cripple Creek, Colorado.

Utah offered a variety of pleasures. In the southern half of the state was a beautiful national park called Capitol Reef. This state park was widely known for its orchards. These orchards had been there for a long time and were cared for by the rangers. When we camped there one summer, we were able to pick as much fruit as we liked. The apricots and cherries were ripe at the time, which happened to be favorites for both of us. The campers used the picnic tables to dry the fruit so they could take it home for the winter, and they also ate as much as they could hold. The latter presented a big problem. The park only had one men's room and one ladies room. There was always a constant line of people waiting to get in – all with bowel problems from eating too many apricots and cherries. There was no other place than Utah where we found so much fresh fruit, or a good cleaning out.

Our next stop was north of Salt Lake City at Promontory Summit, where the Central Pacific Railroad and Union Pacific Railroad companies met to drive in the last spike that connected the first transcontinental railroad on May 10, 1869. Nowadays, they reenact the last spike being nailed into the railroad track with a nice little show, complete with audience participation. Of course, with Bill's long beard and looks, he was quickly chosen for the day's show.

We also visited Dinosaur National Park on the Utah-Colorado border. The park was 210,000 acres and actually located in both Colorado and Utah. We watched as men chipped away lightly in an enclosed area on a mountainside that contained many dinosaur bones. It was fascinating to actually see these bones being unearthed. They also had a shuttle that took people to an old hideout where western outlaws were nursed back to health. The best part was the prairie dogs that popped up in the middle of the dirt road as we drove along in the shuttle. They would sit with their heads popped out of the holes, waiting for the cars to come at them, and then duck down at the last moment.

After our trip through Utah, we traveled north into Idaho to see the Snake River. We found a park along the river that offered white water rafting. Of course we had to try it. A bus took us miles up the river and then we rafted back to the park. The bus ride was as much fun as the raft ride. There was no road. Instead, the bus cut right through the desert, up and down dunes, twisting through mesquite bushes. The bus had to be one of the first ever made. It was amazing it held together. We were literally knocked right out of our seats many times. I believe this was how they let us know what we were in for on the water. When we reached the river, our oarsman was waiting to give us instructions. My first shock was that we did not actually sit in the raft; we sat around the edge of the large tube and held onto a rope for safety, and the oarsman sat on a board across the center. As we put our life jackets on, he explained to us that if we fell out, nothing could be done about it until we got out of the rapids and into calm water. Then, we could be picked up before the next rapid. His main advice was if one of us fell out of the raft we needed to lay flat on our backs so we could kick ourselves off of the rocks instead of hit them with our heads. These were not really rocks, per se. They were boulders sticking out of the water by a good 3 to 4 feet.

As we set off in the raft, Bill told me to keep my feet loose on the canvas floor so they would just rise and fall with it. All was well until I saw the first rapid. Oh my, this was scary. I stupidly braced my feet against the floor as we hit the first rapid, and up in the air flew my feet. With the help of Bill and the rope I was clinging to for dear life, I managed to stay on the raft. On the next rapid I did it right. We took a break from the action on a small beach along some calm waters in the canyon where we were fed a picnic lunch of chicken and watermelon. We all took a swim in our clothes. It no longer mattered because we were already soaking wet. We had a great oarsman who could really handle that raft. We never hit a rock, but we missed quite a few by only a matter of inches. The trip was a memorable ride that I would recommend to anyone if they have the opportunity.

We stayed in Idaho for quite some time and were actually in Hayburn State Park near the Idaho-Washington border when Mt. St. Helens erupted on May 18, 1980. Even though the eruption was on the other side of the state, all the trees were covered in solid ash, and as we walked, the ash was several inches deep everywhere on the ground. It was quite some time before we could actually travel to the other side of the state and get anywhere near the volcano. When we arrived, the site was unbelievable. All of the ash was either a wet sludge or was drying up as hard as cement. The ash rushed down the mountain so fast that we saw a cabin filled from floor to ceiling. As bad as it was a few months after the eruption, I cannot imagine what these people lived through on that day.

After our trip through Washington we stopped along the shoreline in Oregon. It was unlike any of the beaches we had ever seen. The ocean came right up to the edge of the cliffs and the water crashed onto the rocks just a few feet from shore. We enjoyed picking up driftwood on the smaller beaches, which I used in my crafts. It was scary driving on the roads in Oregon near the logging areas. The lumber trucks were really nothing more than trucks pulling a large Redwood tree with wheels strapped to the back to act like a trailer. The trucks roared down the hills, and we knew that if we got in the way we would never have a chance.

When we were near Portland, we tried to find some old friends that we had not seen in more than 25 years named John and Melinda Bishop. John worked with Bill in New Jersey and met his wife in England during the war. At first they had trouble having a baby so they adopted a little girl. It must have helped because after the adoption they went on to have 11 more children of their own. We found out that John was a building inspector in a nearby town so we dropped by his office unannounced and surprised the hell out of him. His first comment was, "Boy, you guys got old." After we visited for awhile, John told us his wife was out shopping. We stopped at the store to see if we could find her. I recognized Melinda looking through a rack of blouses so I walked up to her and said, "Ma'am, you do know you will have to buy any of the blouses you have touched." Thinking I was a salesperson, she really started to give me a piece of her mind. When she was finished I told her I was Mina Moore and she almost fainted. We stayed with them and had dinner, and the next day we drove through the Cascade Range.

We continued traveling south and headed into California to Humboldt County to see the redwood trees. We really felt insignificant standing next to them. The height and density of the trees was overwhelming. The redwoods are different from other trees because they get their nourishment through the bark. We stood inside of one particular tree that was nearly empty on the inside yet the tree itself was growing just as tall as the others. We could barely see the sky through those trees. It was a fascinating place to ride on our motorcycle.

We rode past a lumberjack outing, and stopped to see what was going on. They immediately invited us to stay, which was easy to accept when we saw a half dozen whole prime ribs turning on a big grill. Before we ate, the lumberjacks and their wives competed against each other. This was a very good natured but rough group of people. The women could throw an axe and get a bulls-eye just as well as the men. In one of the contests, the men had to grab the end of a logging chain and drag it to a redwood log that was about 6 feet in diameter and lying on the ground. Next, they had to climb over the log with the chain and drag it to the next log, which was raised off the ground. They had to get the chain around that piece and once again hook back into the chain. Everyone was cheering like crazy. I could not believe it, but when the men were done, the women went next. Those women lugged that chain, especially one gal named Daisy. She was much faster than the other women, and to keep her going at her quick pace the lumberjacks were yelling, "Come on Daisy, bounce those tits." This was down-to-earth fun, and the best food we ever ate. Before we left they wanted to give us a couple of big burls, which are slices out of a redwood log. We could have made beautiful tables out of them but we just did not have the room in our trailer to carry them. Looking back, I would have liked to have some of those for our girls. The lumberjacks we met were some of the hardest working and finest people we ever met during our travels.

Just outside of Oakland, on the east side of the San Francisco Bay, we spent an entertaining day watching college students at the University of California, Berkeley. We climbed up a tree near the campus to get a look at the surrounding area. I know many well-educated students must graduate from there, but from our roost it was more like a three ring circus. The dress code at the time must have been to look as weird as possible. One group was ranting and raving about religion, another group about politics. Then we saw sidewalk psychiatrists offering help. Another barefoot group was flitting around the grass doing some form of dancing. Yet another group was meditating on the lawn. Bill and I just looked at each other in wonder, and no comment needed to be made. We were curious what the tuition fee was for a student to attend Berkley and what they were getting for the money.

I definitely did our wine tour all wrong in Napa Valley. We volunteered to take part in a wine tasting survey. They lined up a glass of wine in front of us and we had to write down our comments. I was the first one they served so I downed each glass and tried to write a comment. I soon noticed that the other people in the group, including

Bill, just swirled it a little, sniffed it, and took a tiny little taste. I was the only one who walked out of there feeling very, very happy. I asked Bill how he knew what to do, and to my surprise he said he saw it in a movie. The stinker let me just down one after another. Good thing I was not the one driving the motorcycle.

When we visited Los Angeles, the one place I wanted to go was to see the Kings play hockey, which was my favorite sport to watch. We went in the afternoon to ask a guard where we should park our cycle for the game. He had us pull our motorcycle right into the side entrance where he was standing guard, and in we walked to watch the game. My helmet with the wig on it always broke the ice and gave us little perks.

Another thrill in Los Angeles was going to see the Rose Parade. To actually see all of those beautiful flower displays was a treat. We left our campsite at 5 a.m. in order to be close to the parade. Many people slept there overnight in sleeping bags on the side of the road. It was cold when we left on the cycle so we dressed in several layers of clothing. As it warmed up throughout the morning, we began peeling them off one by one. Luck was with us and we found a spot right on the road without anyone in front of us, but it did not take long for people to come in swarms. It was so crowded that we could not have moved if we wanted to. By the end of the parade I had to go to the bathroom so badly, I was desperate. I asked a lady standing near us if she knew of a bathroom close by. She said we could go around the corner to the gas station parking lot where their motor home was parked and use their bathroom. The door was open, which I thought was odd. I ran over to her motor home, walked in, and found her husband watching the parade on television. I just went right into the bathroom, came out, said "thank you" and left. You should have seen the look on his face: He was stunned but the look was priceless. I repeat, I was really desperate and I had to go. I could only hope his wife explained to him about the crazy lady who walked in, used the bathroom, and left.

Bill got the opportunity to take me to the San Diego Zoo just like he said years before when he came home from the war. We also stopped at Balboa Park in San Diego, which featured many attractions. We were impressed with an art museum there, where we walked along a red carpet past a gold roped-in walkway. The docents were dressed in tuxedos. I did Bill proud because I was very ladylike, which I could actually be when it was necessary.

After our trip to San Diego, we decided to cross the border again to visit Tijuana. We had a little problem coming back into the United States. Going in was easy but coming out was a little nerve racking. We rode our cycle through the checkpoint but were then flagged down. A couple of Mexican policemen came running after us blowing their whistles. We pulled over to the side of the road where they searched us and took parts of our bike apart. I guess they were looking for drugs. This time I guess my wig-helmet made me look too much like a hippie and got us into a little trouble. They were satisfied and let us go after we put our motorcycle back together.

Our next stops in California were though the desert areas of the state. The first place we visited was Palm Springs. There is nothing better than a date shake in Palm Springs. They are fattening but delicious. We also spotted Elizabeth Taylor shopping in one of Palm Springs' exclusive boutiques. We strolled in wearing our usual attire and were more or less ignored. The place was exquisite but had no merchandise in sight. Everything was modeled for patrons as they sat and enjoyed martinis. I wonder if they would have modeled jeans for us.

When we drove through Death Valley it was incredibly hot. We were traveling with the camper and pulled over near a picnic bench to eat. All of our windows were wide open to try and cool the trailer a little bit as we ate our supper. We had just sat down when out of nowhere a dust storm sprang up like I had never seen in my life. In seconds our hair, faces, and dinner were covered with dust. Bill shouted, "Oh no, the windows!" We ran into the camper and there were hills of dust piled by each window. We cleaned off the picnic table and slept on it because we could not stay inside. We waited until morning to tackle the clean up job on the camper. We collected enough sand to have our own private sand dune. We rode through all of Death Valley, which was quite a desolate place, and wound up in Las Vegas. We stayed in Las Vegas for a week and decided we would like to spend a little more time there.

Our next goal was to see Alaska. We were deciding whether to do it with the camper or with the cycle and trailer when we got a call from Mina, our youngest daughter. She was very upset and getting a divorce.

She asked us to come back to Pennsylvania. We agreed to come back but we had to go slow because it was winter and riding in snow and ice with our camper was not one of our favorite ideas. By the time we made it back to Pennsylvania, she was divorced and fairly well settled. We stayed in Pennsylvania for the summer but headed back to Las Vegas before the bad weather started up again. Unfortunately, we never did get to Alaska.

Through our travels, we never planned on settling anywhere permanently. However, when we stayed in Las Vegas, we soon realized this could be a city where we could stay for quite some time. Plus it was close to some of the most beautiful sights in the country like the Grand Canyon and Bryce Canyon. In the early 1980s, Las Vegas was an extremely affordable town to live in. As frugally as we lived, we still managed to live pretty high on the hog (for us anyway) in Las Vegas. Although we loved settling down for a few years, we never meant it to be long term. However, fate stepped in and changed my life when Bill was taken from me. To this day, even in my 80s, if I were able to drive, I would still be roaming the country. Instead, I now travel with Bill in my mind through the wonderful memories we collected during 20 years of active "retirement."

Chapter 10
LAS VEGAS

In 1984 after visiting Las Vegas, we decided to make it our home for a while. The city could only be properly described as fantasyland for adults. In the early 1980's, the city was considerably smaller, with a population in Las Vegas and the surrounding area of less than a half million people. Besides the obvious lights, glitz, and glamour of the city, we had to get used to the treeless mountains and desert landscaping surrounding most of the homes. Although we missed the trees, there are very few things in this world more beautiful than the sun rising or setting over the mountains in the Las Vegas valley.

Unlike the mega resorts that have taken over the Las Vegas Strip, when we moved to town it was considerably smaller and quieter. The MGM Grand, Mirage, and Bellagio were still many years away. The main hotels were Caesars Palace, Tropicana, Flamingo, and the Stardust. The downtown section was kind of a honky-tonk area with girls on the sidewalk trying to offer coupons to pedestrians to try and get them in their casinos. Traffic at the time was not that bad and we managed to ride our motorcycle in the city without any problems. One of our favorite hobbies was going out to the buffets for many of our meals. When Circus Circus was offering forty-five breakfast selections for a $1.49, why bother cooking at home.

Today Las Vegas has become more mainstream and accepted as a regular city. Now tourists in Las Vegas can ride a gondola through a casino, see white tigers in another, and watch an erupting volcano every 15 minutes. Dolphins swim in their own luxurious habitat and circus acts fly overhead as people gamble and pirates sink a ship on the strip. I have not been back to Las Vegas since 1996. Although the explosive growth of the casino industry started when we lived in the city, I do no think I would recognize the place I once lived. Our old hangouts such as the Sands, Dunes, Desert Inn, and the Hacienda have become distant memories and made way for the Venetian, Bellagio, Wynn Las Vegas, and Mandalay Bay.

When we lived in Las Vegas for 10 years, for $2.50 a drink we could see name entertainers at the lounge shows and as locals we would get coupons for two for one buffet's at prices ranging from $4.99 to $8.95. Some of the hotels would still let locals swim at their pools. Now the city and surrounding areas has a population of more than 1.7 million residents and expands into areas of the desert that did not even have a single road when we moved to the city.

Aside from the gaming aspect, we loved all of the other activities Las Vegas had to offer. One of the "local" hotels, the Sante Fe, had an ice skating rink where we would go to watch peewee teams play hockey. All we could see on the ice was an oversized uniform with a little face showing through the mask. The kids would be skating on their ankles after the puck, and then take a shot miss it completely when they finally got there. We cheered them on, and they were stars in their own mind.

When we first stayed in Las Vegas, we parked our camper at an RV Park adjacent to Sam's Town Hotel & Casino off Boulder Highway. When we decided to first settle down in Las Vegas, we took a job working in a laundromat on Tropicana Avenue so we could have some fun money. This laundromat also did dry cleaning and ironing. Bill got the job doing the dry cleaning and I told them I would do the ironing for no wages, just so we could work together. They were happy to do this and so were we. It turned out many of the people who played in bands as well as showgirls and entertainers would often need some repairs in a hurry, such as a button sewed on or a ripped seam, and I was always happy to oblige. They gave me such big tips that many days I actually earned more than Bill. We did this job for a year when I read in the paper that a large construction company needed someone with a camper to act as 24-hour security in the equipment yard. We applied and got the job. We were in our own fenced in area with two big sheds and a covered patio. We were not paid for staying in the yard, but in exchange the company covered the rent plus all utilities including phone. This was a great deal for both parties. We no longer had to work and with social security and free living we could do fine. We stayed as security guards at this site for 10 years.

Now that we had some security and were settled down in Las Vegas, I could concentrate on making more headway on my own. Although my panic attacks were not as prevalent during our years of traveling, they were still always in my mind. One of the ways we started to deal with my problem was by going to a casino and playing separate games. Bill always loved to play blackjack and I would play nickel poker machines. I would roam the casino on my own and then find the table Bill played on. At first I would look for him in about 15 minutes. But I kept working at staying alone at a poker machine and over time I got better at it until I could stay as long as I felt like playing and then I would go look for Bill. If he went broke first, instead of looking for me he would give me some room and stay by a table and watch the game until I would come looking for him.

Next we tried shopping. We went to a two-story mall in the city. Bill sat on a bench by a pretzel stand and I roamed as far as possible, knowing he would never move from his spot. After all of these years together, I still could not believe how frightened I was simply walking away from him. After many weeks of practice, I was able to roam on my own for up to an hour. Bill's comment was, "Now I am going to have to give you some shopping money, since you've become a shopper.'

Bill had promised me that if we stopped roaming around the country I could get a dog. For three weeks I saw the same ad in the paper, "Special person needed to adopt a blind, mistreated, one year old Australian Shepherd." On the third week that Bill saw me reading the same ad he said, "why don't you get her, you know you want her." So we did. Bill named her Sweetie. It took Sweetie about a month to come out from under the bed. Once she knew she could trust us not to hurt her she really made headway. If we moved anything I only had to take her to it, let her smell it, and I would hit the object saying careful, and she would go around it from then on. She would play hide and go seek with me outside. We also had a long telephone pole laying down in our yard that she could walk along the top of and she never fell off.

As a special treat we took her to Mt. Charleston, which is only a half hour from Las Vegas. On the mountain she got to feel her first snow. At first she walked rather funny in it, but later took her head and dug it in the snow. On another trip to Mt. Charleston we camped in the truck and had a picnic on the edge of the woods. Sweetie's ears perked up and she sat very still. In a little while we heard a sound but had no idea what it was until out of nowhere eight wild horses came running through the woods just a few feet from us. It sounded like a whole herd stomping by our picnic.

A Las Vegas news reporter saw us with Sweetie in the parking lot of a supermarket and asked if he could put her on television. He was amazed that we had left Sweetie in the car with some other bags of groceries and she was so well trained that she did not touch a single bag. When he found out she was blind, he decided to do a story on us. He came over to our place with all his equipment and filmed her for hours. Bill and I were also interviewed for the piece and we discussed how well a blind dog could adapt if only people would spend a little time with them.

Bill and I lived on Tropicana Avenue about a half-mile west of Las Vegas Boulevard. We headed out on the motorcycle and decided to go to Sam's Town for a Mexican dinner. Sam's Town is at the eastern end of Tropicana about six miles from our place. Once we crossed The Strip I asked Bill something but he did not answer me. I tried to speak to him a few more times but he did not respond. Since I had been living with his diabetes for so many years I knew what to do. I pulled out a Fig Newton that I usually carried with me for just an occasion and gave it to him. Instead of eating it, he threw it on the side of the road. Now I knew we had a problem. A block before Sam's Town I yelled, "Pull over, pull over, I'm sick." For some reason he pulled over to the side of the road and stopped. I practically shoved the Fig Newton down his throat. When he became himself again, I asked what he remembered last. He said, "Crossing the Strip and after that everything is blank." That was almost six miles back. Since Las Vegas can be bumper-to-bumper traffic with a stop light at every block on Tropicana, it could have become an extremely dangerous situation. On that ride Bill stopped at everything light and followed along with the traffic like everything was normal. I think it was amazing because he was driving only by instinct. With all that traffic, we were going slowly enough that I could have jumped off the bike at anytime without hurting myself. But then what would have happened to Bill if he slipped further into a seizure while driving the motorcycle alone? All ended well after he pulled over and ate the Fig Newton and we enjoyed our dinner at Willie and Jose's inside of Sam's Town.

We had lived in Las Vegas for a few years when we finally decided it was time to sell our motorcycle. The final straw was one summer day when Bill and I were stuck in some bumper-to-bumper traffic and the temperature was well above 100 degrees. By the time we got home, we were both so sick we knew our motorcycling days in the city were over. Our pickup was also getting pretty old and had served us well, but with the camper parked at the construction yard, it was not going anywhere. So we sold the motorcycle and purchased a Subaru pickup that was very easy to maneuver around the city. We added a fiberglass cap so Sweetie could sit in the back, but she always seemed to find her way to the front seat with us.

I always had two desires in my life. One was to oil paint and the other was to work with Special Olympics. The senior center in Las Vegas had an oil painting class once a week for $1 per lesson. I joined, worked very hard at it, and learned how to paint. I practiced my craft for four years before I had the courage to enter two paintings in an art show. One was a portrait of old Eskimo I had patterned from the cover of a National Geographic magazine. The other was a portrait of a long horn sheep on a mountainside. It was a mixed message at the art show. Unfortunately both paintings were stolen from the show. However, they were the only ones stolen so I could take that as a positive in regards to the quality of my work. Since then I have created many different styles of paintings. I enjoy painting with a palette knife instead of a brush, so it gives the artwork a unique look. I often get to use them as gifts for weddings or birthdays.

From 1988 to 1993 we fulfilled my second desire. We became coaches for the Special Olympics. We taught bowling, softball, swimming, and basketball. Those 6 years were some of the most fulfilling years of our life. These mentally and physically handicapped people were so loving and dedicated; yet so challenged that we all could learn from them. All of the children had a wonderful attitude. Maybe they did not have the proper technique, but it never kept them from trying again and again. Like any team, we did have a few shining stars. We even had two bowlers that could break 200 every so often.

Our joy was seeing the kids enjoy themselves, no matter the sport. We coached one little girl in basketball that could not hold her balance, but she wanted to play so bad, we had to figure out a plan. Instead of letting her run by herself and possibly get hurt, I held her hand tightly and together we played as one person on the team. Bill enjoyed the coaching as well but most of the time he would be busy trying to get the other kids to dribble the ball as they ran down the court.

When we coached softball, we had just as much fun. We had one player, Mike, that insisted on running the bases in reverse when he hit the ball. We had to make a rule change for him because he could not comprehend the difference. It was an adventure as a coach when Mike is running from third to second to first to home while Tony just stayed on second and decided not to run. This means that Amy who was on first, runs past Tony on second and goes to third base. Now this play beats Abbot and Costello's, "Who's on First, What's on Second" any day of the week.

My heart will always go out to Mary, one of our swimmers, who had been mentally and physically abused to the point her left arm and leg were partially paralyzed. She wanted so badly to swim, but when she tried she would just sink to the bottom. I talked to her for a long time and explained that she had to find a way to push herself up for air when she sank to the bottom. I asked her if she trusted me to try something and she replied, "Grandma you won't let me drown, I know that." So I told her when she sinks to the bottom, I would be there for her but she must find a way to get herself up to the top using her good side. She not only accomplished this, but also learned to swim and over time was able to compete with the Special Olympics swim team. She swam in the lane closest to the edge of the pool so I could walk along with her. I will never forget what a big smile she had on her face. And there I was crying my head off because I was so proud of her.

The Special Olympics coordinators were able to use the college swimming pool on the campus of UNLV. Bill handled the better swimmers in the deep end of the pool and even had them diving off the low board. Inevitably the diving turned into cannon balls and Bill usually seemed to be right in the thick of it with the kids.

Each Saturday night the Special Olympics volunteers planned a dance party. As I said before Bill was not a dancer but he always danced with the athletes and me every Saturday night. To say we danced is stretching a point. It was more like jumping, hopping, turning round and round, but they loved it.

One afternoon our kids were invited to walk into the Silver Bowl, where the UNLV football team played, before a game. They escorted athletes receiving awards for their particular sports. The event was organized so our special athletes walked with someone that participated in the same sport. It turned out to be hysterical because our athletes figured the applause and cheers were for them. They hogged the show by bowing, saluting, and waving to the audience and glowing in the glory of it all. We never told them any different: why bust their bubble, they deserved it. If you ever want to feel the deepest, sincerest love and devotion that is possible, then become a coach for the Special Olympics.

One of our other highlights living in Las Vegas was spending a day on the set of a movie as an extra. In 1986, Sylvester Stallone filmed a movie called, "Over the Top." Our scene was filmed at the Las Vegas Hilton. We were in the crowd cheering during the arm wrestling competition. In the final version of the movie, Bill can be seen clear as day because he stood out with his beard. I was right next to him but I was cut out of the film. When the camera would pan by they kept telling us not to look directly into the camera. Of course I could not listen so that is probably why I ended up on the cutting room floor. Bill scene is during the final arm wrestling match at the end of the movie.

While living in Las Vegas, each of our four grandchildren came to visit us at different times. It seemed like each visit had its own adventure. John, our oldest, grandchild, came to visit before going to UCLA for a seminar on filmmaking. He stayed with us for a few days and then we drove him to California. We camped at Bear Lake where Bill and I stayed in the truck cap and John slept in a sleeping bag outside. The next day we went for a swim in the lake. When I got out of the water I took a sip from an open soda can I had left on the shore. Much to my shock, a bee had crawled inside the can and flew out and stung me in the mouth. This hurt terribly and started to swell up immediately. Luckily it did not make it to my throat or could have really been in trouble.

When Julie and Eric came to visit we packed up the truck with a tent for the kids and headed for the Grand Canyon. That evening we stayed at a campsite near the canyon and I decided to set up for breakfast at night so we could get an early start in the morning. I had a picnic table set up with the stove and all of the food in the icebox so we could get a quick start and not waste any time when we woke up. When we woke up in the morning, we discovered it had snowed two inches that night and the picnic table was covered in a blanket of snow. The stove was wet and would not light so instead of a nice warm breakfast we sat freezing in the tent and had cold milk and graham crackers. To liven up the morning, Eric made a snowman as a centerpiece on the picnic table.

Dan came out to visit right before he graduated from high school and we were not aware he had never camped before. We made an overnight trip to see Zion Canyon and Bryce Canyon in Utah. We arrived at the campground and Bill and I once again stayed in the back of the truck but Dan was not too keen about sleeping on the ground among the wildlife. To ease his mind, we set his sleeping bag on top of the picnic table. It did not take long for Dan to be tapping on the window and asking if he could sleep inside the truck with us. While laying in his sleeping bag he heard some rustling sounds by a tree. He flicked on a flashlight and found himself staring at a skunk. That was enough nature for him so he was in the truck with us. To make matters worse Dan also had not worn socks in his sneakers all week so the smell from his shoes may have caused us to pass out.

In early 1990 my daughter Mina and her second husband, Ron, decided to move to Las Vegas after visiting us from Pennsylvania. Since I was feeling more confident in my ability to go out alone, I was able to take my next step and go out for a day with Mina. During one of our first outings we stopped at a store where the show people sold their clothes on consignment. We saw this $2000 evening dress that Mina wanted me to try on just for fun. I wiggled into it but I did not think it did anything for me. However, then I had to take it off. Much to my surprise, we could not get it over my boobs. Between starting to sweat, laughing our heads off, and Mina pushing my boobs every which way I finally got it off without ripping it. If the dress had ripped the sales clerk would have seen two females running as fast as they could away from that store.

On another day out with Mina, we decided to go to the Debbie Reynolds Casino to see Debbie's show at the hotel. During the show, we were actually interacting with her and doing a little audience to stage kidding during the performance. Only in Vegas: we wound up on stage with Debbie Reynolds and the three of us were singing "Three Little Fishes." I could not believe I was brave enough to get on stage in front of all of those people.

In the summer of 1990 Mina's youngest son Dan moved to Las Vegas as well to attend college at UNLV. Since we did not get to see Dan play in Little League, we made up for it by watching him play softball for his fraternity team. It did not take long for Bill and I to become one of the gang and hang out with all of his friends at the game. During one game in particular, Dan made an outstanding play and I yelled out "that's my baby." Of course after that every time he made a good play all his friends and I yelled "that's my baby." Dan couldn't do much about it except say an "oh no." We got close to Dan and since we left Pennsylvania when he was young, the softball games were a little like reliving his childhood, except it now contained beer drinking by the players and fans.

In 1991 my brother moved out to Las Vegas from Cape Cod after his wife had a stroke. She was not doing well and ended up having to be placed in a nursing home. My brother Bill did his best, but he hard a hard time dealing with the situation. She was very difficult to deal with and ended up being severely medicated just to keep her calm.

I got a big surprise in 1994 on my 70th birthday when a stretch limousine pulled up to our place. The chauffer handed me red roses and we drank champagne inside. Our driver had a great sense of humor. First he pulled into a McDonald's then said "oops wrong place." He turned us into several not so nice places until he finally arrived at the front door of Caesar's Palace. When we stopped, he opened my door, helped me out, leaned me way back and gave me a big kiss at the foot of the steps to Caesar's. Inside we were escorted to the "Bachanal Room," which was the best restaurant in the hotel. Each table had at least four girls in Egyptian costumes to wait on us. Other Egyptian girls danced continually around a huge fountain. The girls kept our wine glasses full and for an added bonus, they dipped grapes into the wine and fed them to my awe struck husband. Bill also received a neck message from a very scantly dressed girl who rested his head on her bosom. My Bill almost died of embarrassment. I just laughed and told him to enjoy because it would not be happening again. During dessert, Caesar and Cleopatra came dressed in their fabulous regalia. Caesar kissed each ladies hand and he gave her a bottle of Cleopatra perfume. I don't know what Cleopatra was doing I was too interested in Caesar. All this was a wonderful surprise given to me by my daughter and her husband on my 70th birthday. Now the motto for the city is "What happens in Vegas, stays in Vegas." It was also going on 10 years prior to the saying becoming famous.

Although we enjoyed our life in Las Vegas, Bill was starting to develop heart problems. It was to be expected after living over 30 years with diabetes, even though he rigidly controlled his insulin. The medical bills and medication started to take a toll on us financially, so I decided to supplement our money by hand decorating home made Ukrainian eggs. I took a class at a senior center in Las Vegas on how to decorate the eggs. The process was quite intricate and time consuming. First I drew the design on the egg with a pencil. The original design was hand drawn and could be anything I wanted. First I dipped the egg in yellow dye. Then I covered everything that I wanted to be yellow in bees wax and used an electric heating tool to dry the wax. Then I dipped the egg in red dye and rubbed wax on this area. I kept going until the entire egg was covered in wax. After that I put the egg in a toaster over and waiting for the wax to melt. When the wax started to melt I quickly took it out of the oven and rubbed the wax off with a paper towel. This had to been done fast so the egg inside did not cook. After I finished removing the wax, I made a tiny hole with a fine drill in each end of the shell and blew the egg out of the inside. This always gave me a headache because I had to blow pretty hard into a small area just to get the egg to come out the other side. After the egg was cleaned out I sprayed it with an acrylic to give it a shiny gloss. By using this process I could make three eggs each night. I sold hundreds of the eggs ranging from $7.00 to $15.00 per piece depending on the intricacy. I sold most of the eggs at the hospital where Mina was a nurse, and it helped cover the medicine Bill needed.

In early 1995 we had to move from our home because a casino was going to be built on the lot. Not long after we moved, Bill was hospitalized after suffering a heart attack. Shortly after he was released, he also had a minor stroke. All of the years of taking insulin and living with diabetes were taking a toll on his body. When he got out he made me promise not to hospitalize him again, but keep him home. I promised him I would. Bill's health was rapidly declining and the doctors told us he had about three months left, but he held out for eight. He even bowled three days before he died. Bill accepted the short time he had and never talked about himself. Instead he worried about me and told me over and over that I could do it and that I was strong enough to be alone. I hear those words often now and I am determined to prove him right.

In late September, sadly we lost Sweetie. Her hind legs gave out and she had to be put to sleep. The next week, on Bill's birthday, we were preparing to move to a campground the next day so I would be set up if something happened. That day Bill received a card from Sandra thanking him for all the special things he did for her in her lifetime. She must have listed dozens and dozens of nice things. He felt very good about that and remarked how nice it was she remembered so much from our past. The girls each gave Bill $50.00 to play blackjack with on his birthday. That evening we went to a casino to have some fun. I had won a $200.00 jackpot on a nickel machine and hurried to tell Bill. When I saw him he was on the floor with medics working on him, but he was gone. He died on October 1st, 1995, his 72nd birthday, and my heart broke that same day. The next morning I had to move by myself to campground with the help of Mina and Ron. That morning as I packed to leave my way of coping was to throw everything in a dumpster. I looked at my paint supplies said, "I'll never paint again" so in the dumpster it went. I did this with half the stuff I owned. I don't know why, it just was my way at that instant to try and ease the pain.

As he wished, Bill was cremated and his ashes are still with me. Someday when I join him again, our ashes will be spread together in the rose garden at the Indiantown Gap Military Cemetery in Pennsylvania.

Mina, Ron, Dan, his girlfriend and I had a memorial service for Bill. I told Sandra not to come out at that time, but to wait three months when I knew the shock was going to wear off and I was going to need her. She did just that and I was so glad to see her when she arrived. Sandra helped me so much at my new place. I had no phone connection on my site so we dug across the road to the other side where there were connections. Now I at least had a phone. I wanted to sell our truck because I did not drive. We could not sell the truck in its current condition because the headlights did not work. Sandra fixed the headlights so we were able to sell the truck.

The best advice she gave me was suggesting I get a cat. We went to a pet store and this gray cat was crouched in the corner of a cage. When I saw her in the cage she walked towards me and stared me right in the eyes, as if to say "we both need each other badly." Sandra and I both felt it and we went to pieces. I took kitty home and we were so good for each other. She was so special and Kitty was with me for eight years until she became incurably sick. I just could not replace her since she got me through the worst of my grieving.

After Sandra had to return home, my granddaughter Julie came out three months later and stayed with me for a while. It felt so good having company and we really had a nice time eating out and going to shows. In the end I only stayed in Las Vegas for a year after I lost Bill. My doctor and my brother both advised me to move out of Las Vegas and try to make a life for myself somewhere else. It was the right move for me. Everything in Las Vegas reminded me of my husband. I was never going to improve living with the painful reminders of the city everyday. Sandra called me in late September to tell me about a little house she found for me in Forest City, Pennsylvania. The house was about 15 minutes from where she lived and was perfect for me. I knew I would never heal in Las Vegas so I had to try something else to ease the uncontrollable grief.

Chapter 11
LIFE IN PENNSYLVANIA

My son-in-law Mark flew into Las Vegas to drive me back to Pennsylvania. I was returning to a place where I had not lived in 21 years. I rented a U-Haul, took my new refrigerator as well as a bed, television, table, two chairs, a platform rocker, along with clothes, dishes, and personals items from the camper. I asked a fellow in the area to help me with moving out and in return I gave him the camper. He was thrilled to have a place to move in to with his girlfriend. On October 1, 1996, exactly a year after I lost Bill, Mark arrived and we left the same day for Pennsylvania.

My brother came along with us to help me get acclimated to my new home. His wife no longer recognized him so the nursing home told him it would do him some good to get away for a month. Kitty of course was also with us. She rode the whole time wrapped around the back of my neck. It took us four days, staying in a motel each night.

I was very pleased when I saw my new home. It is a little one-story house with four rooms upstairs and a basement. The house is perfect for one person with a good-sized kitchen, front room, bedroom, and spare room. It also has enough property to plant a garden of what I like, but not too much for me to handle. I also have a tool shed in back and a small barn. Sandra scrounged around the area and found some used furniture such end tables, television and stand, two dressers, a desk, a nightstand, and a folding bed. She also found furniture for my enclosed front porch. The local flea market supplied everything else I needed like curtains, yard tools, and a wheelbarrow for a very low price. My brother Bill spend his time at my new home unpacking, arranging the furniture, and getting familiar with the area. Sandra loaned Bill one of their cars so we were all set to learn our surroundings.

Forest City was a booming mining town of almost 6,000 people in the early 1900's. A large vein of anthracite coal ran all the way from Wilkes Barre up through Forest City. The entire area is dotted with small towns similar to Forest City that sprung up during the peak of the mines. The coal was close to the surface near Forest City and the mine ran right under the town. The entrance to the mine was less than a block from Main Street. In the 1920's the coal started to run out and one by one the mines started to close. By the 1960's very few of the mines in Northeastern Pennsylvania were in operation.

By the 1990's the population in the area had dwindled to less than 2,000 residents and our quaint little town looked very similar to many in Northeastern Pennsylvania. The town is based around Main Street and consists of many vacant stores, plus a florist, town newspaper, doctor, dentist, car dealer, and senior center. I cannot go anywhere in Forest City without walking up or down a steep hill. Within walking distance from my home, I found Kennedy Park. This is where the little leagues play, plus it has tennis courts and a good size pond where we swim regularly during the summer.

Every Wednesday my brother Bill and I would go to town and do my shopping plus go to the Post Office, pay bills, and eat lunch out. Of course we would stop and talk to the storeowners and other shoppers. Bill and I enjoyed the town because the people were so friendly. A new person in an old little town sticks out like a sore thumb. All the people here went to school together, and many are somehow related to one another. Forest City is also a predominantly old school Catholic neighborhood. Since I am Lutheran, I was a little surprised how easily I assimilated into the town and the people welcomed me. My biggest problem in the neighborhood was the people in the town only had one new name to remember, but I had the whole town's to learn. I still get everyone mixed up, especially when their names are Russian, Polish, or Slovenian, but we all manage.

The real blessing, since I cannot drive, is the town has a senior shuttle bus that picks me up at my house any Monday, Wednesday, or Friday for a quarter. That same shuttle will also takes people for doctor visits or to the mall, K-mart, or Wal-Mart which is a good half hour away for only $1 round trip. The bus runs from 9:00 to 2:30 and picks us up when we are done and take us back right to our house. This convenience made a big difference in my life. I can come and go without having to depend on anyone. Independence is very important to me. I usually take the shuttle every Monday to Scranton just to get out among people and shop around.

After a month, Bill left and headed back to Las Vegas. He hated to go since he liked living in a small town instead of a big city. Now it was time for me to settle in and make a life for myself. The only way I can describe what it was like to live without my husband was I spent the first five years crying every day. What else could I do since I shared such an incredible journey with Bill for 52 years, and all of a sudden he was gone? I don't think anyone would expect me to react any differently. I just ignored the crying and let it come out while I tried to continue on.

The best therapy for my problem was to keep busy. The first year I repainted the whole inside of my house. I also added some stenciling in each room to give it a nice touch. Next I tackled the furniture. Much of it was used and in need of a little tender loving care, so I refinished the wood on many of the pieces. Then I painted the bedroom furniture white. When I completed the project it looked like I had a new bedroom set. I did not have a house to play with for 25 years so the newness of a house was good for me. Also, it was my home in a new place, so I was not constantly reminded of my husband by every piece of furniture or with the house. He was always on my mind but that was thinking about our memories together. It might be hard to understand, but to me there is a big difference between fondly remembering something in the past as opposed to being constantly reminded of something by my surroundings.

It also helped that I have wonderful neighbors on my street. On my left, I have two elderly bachelors who owned this house when I moved back to Pennsylvania. On my right is a widow in her seventies that is a good friend. They would say to me, "You couldn't sleep last night. We saw your cellar light on at three in the morning. What were you painting this time?" I just about had the inside all looking cozy so the next year I started on the outside. My brother came for vacations to help me. The windows needed painting and I had siding put on the shed. Next we painted the little barn red and I made red shutters and scalping under all the windows. Now the outside of the house looked as good as the inside.

My next feat was to try to go to Carbondale on my own. This is a small town about 15 minutes away by the shuttle, where I could shop for food. No one can understand how difficult that was to do if they do not understand my affliction. I broke out in a sweat, but all the way I was thinking, "Stick with me Bill, you said I could do it." When I got home I felt so good about myself that I knew I would keep doing it until it was no longer a problem. Now I go regularly and think I am a big cheese.

The following year I wanted to work on the yard around the house. Sandra approached my neighbors who owned this house and asked if we could buy it from them. They agreed because they really liked me as their neighbor, and that assured I would stay. Sandra owns seven houses in Forest City that she rents out, so I can do whatever I want with this place. My first project was to remove part of the lawn and add a garden. Working outside in the garden has been wonderful therapy for me. I grow tomatoes, onions, lettuce, cucumbers, kale, string beans, squash, peppers, and eggplants. Since I started the gardening, I have added a strawberry patch, rhubarb, currants, and raspberries. In addition, I have planted many flowerbeds and developed a small bird sanctuary on a small patch in the backyard next to the porch. I can sit on the porch and watch the birds eat. It is filled with shrubbery and three types of bird feeders for the many assorted birds that visit my yard. I also added a gated arbor at the edge of the vegetable garden where hummingbirds gather to feed on the honeysuckle nectar. Since I now live in a rural area, it became necessary to add a good sized fenced around the vegetable garden to keep the deer out that wander into the backyard from time to time.

In 1999 my brother's wife died. Shortly after this, he left Las Vegas and moved permanently to Forest City. He moved into the Penn Apartments, which was designed as low income housing for seniors in the area. It is a very nice place with no maintenance problems and rent includes all utilities and is based on income. We both like to be independent. Although we spend a lot of time together we both want our independence and separate dwellings. In the winter we play shuffleboard once a week and then have dinner out. Bill stops in at least every other day. I am not sure, but sometimes I think Bill only drops by to see my dog Rosie instead of me. During the summer we work in the garden together and go fishing. Bill is 85 years old now but still gets around and even drives although his legs are causing him problems. I like to eat so cooking is a must for me. I always have Bill over when I am making one of his favorites dishes like eggplant or corn on the cob. I never liked to do the dishes, but I have no choice since I it is only me and I never had a dishwasher, except my girls. To be truthful, I never really thought about a dishwasher and now for one person it certainly does not seem necessary.

I tried to go on several vacations with my daughter Sandy and I appreciated her bringing me along. For one trip, we traveled to Chicago to see her son. Another time we visited Cape Cod and stayed with my niece (Bill's daughter). Bill came along with us once when we took a trip to Maryland to visit my grandson and his wife. I found these trips to be hard on me. First of all I did all the traveling in my life with my Bill so not having him with me was very disheartening. Second as any widow will attest to, I felt like a fifth wheel tagging along on any trip no matter where I was going. After a couple of trips, I decided I was going to limit my time away from home. Instead of traveling, I decided to take my life in the opposite direction. I found a wonderful dog to share my home so now I no longer have a reason to travel. I did not mind being tied down in the least. I did all my traveling with my Bill and now I have a dog to keep me company.

I found Rosie, who at the time was an 8-month-old shitzu. Sandra's neighbor raised them and I went to their house to look for a dog to keep me company. One of the puppies ran over to me and wanted to be picked up. She cuddled right up to me and snuggled her head under my chin. That did it. It was love at first sight and she came home with me that day.

What a difference Rosie has made in my life. I have never met a more lovable dog. Now I do not cry nearly as often and once again I have someone who showers me with love every minute of the day. I also no longer come home to an empty house. I never feel lonesome eating with someone begging for a taste the whole time I eat. The best part is I have someone to lie next to me in my bed every night. Rosie curls right up as close as possible. Actually I only wind up with a very small part of the bed by morning.

I mainly will not be traveling very often because I refuse to put Rosie in a kennel. It would be too traumatic for her. Now it takes her two days to get over me leaving her at the dog groomer for an hour. We are extremely attached to one another. Quite frankly she is my main reason for getting up every day. I also walk her twice a day, which is very good for both of us. She is only 20 pounds but she is very protective of me on our walks. If any dog, no matter the size, walks by she will growl at them as if to say, "Don't you go near my Mommy." I would like to tell anyone living alone that an animal can be great comfort.

Rosie and Kitty got along real well while they were together. In 2003 I lost Kitty to an incurable intestinal problem. Sandra wanted me to get another cat right away but I could not think of it. Kitty was a very special cat to me who I swear understood my loss of Bill and tried hard to help me through it. I did raise finch birds for a while. I had 12 of them at one time and I enjoyed watching them hatch out of eggs that were smaller than jellybeans and grow so fast I felt like I could actually watch them grow.

I do manage to stay busy every day. I joined an acting company in town for a couple of years when I could do a comedy part. We put dinner shows on in town. I also read to children under the age of 5 at the library and I still attend a paint class. I also like to help out with town parades and street parties. At home I have Rosie, gardening, jig saw puzzles, and I love to read fiction and non-fiction books. I also like to watch television when an old movie is on. I feel that I have made my Bill proud of me. I also go to the mall now on our senior shuttle bus, which is a good half hour bus ride. While I walk in the mall at some point I always look up and say "Honey do you see me now, I am queen of the mall."

I am now in my 80's and it has been more than 10 years since I lost my Bill. Of course I still miss him as much as ever. I talk to him a lot but I am much more at peace with life. I enjoy my home, gardening, and Rosie. I get lonesome sometimes but never bored. My grandson, Dan, talked me into the project of writing this book. It took about a year just to complete the first draft. Once I got started I found it to be a wonderful experience, to relive my life with Bill. This book gave me the opportunity to laugh at times and cry at others, but I will always feel thankful for the love we shared between us.

As the minister said on that rainy day in Florida on March 21, 1943 "To love and to cherish till death do us part."

I found this poem as part of an obituary in the newspaper. It really describes my life the past 10 years.

> One or the other must leave,
> One or the other must stay.
> One or the other must grieve,
> That is forever the way.
> That is the vow that was sworn,
> Faithful 'til death do us part.
> Braving what had to be borne,
> Hiding the aches in the heart.
> One, howsoever adored,
> First must be summoned away,
> That is the will of the lord,
> One or the other must stay.

Author Unknown

To my Bill:

THANK YOU FOR EVERY DAY.

Epilogue
MY BROTHER'S LIFE IN PENNSYLVANIA

Sadly, my brother passed away on May 25, 2006 and did not get to read the final version of this book. Bill had moved to Forest City, Pennsylvania a few years after me when his wife passed away in 1999. He lived in an apartment complex designed for low-income senior citizens that bases the rent and utilities on the client's current income levels. Since the passing of his wife in a nursing home drained most of his remaining income, he lived at the apartment quite inexpensively. Bill used to stop by almost every day. I used to kid him that visiting me was really just an excuse to see my dog Rosie. Those two were the closest of friends and Rosie would start jumping around when she saw Bill's car pull into the driveway.

My brother and I had a wonderful time together in Pennsylvania. We worked on my vegetable garden during the summer and we fished, picked berries, and played shuffleboard. Whenever the town had a celebration, we would always go together. Bill loved the parades on the 4th of July in Forest City. I was always impressed to see my brother, 60 years removed from his tour of duty, immediately come to attention and salute the flag with such pride and dignity when any military personnel would march by in the parade.

After a few years of talking about traveling, I finally convinced my brother to go out and see the world and enjoy himself with the money he had left. His first desire was to see Australia and New Zealand once again. He told me that he had always felt at home with the Australians. In 2001 he finally conjured up enough courage and flew half way around the world. Even though he could not locate any of his Australian war buddies, he took several day trips throughout the country and enjoyed himself immensely. He then headed over to Port Moresby in New Guinea only to find it had become a bustling city, far removed from the jungle outpost of the 1940's. The jungle airstrips no longer existed, and maybe that was for the best. Bill did not need to relive all of those memories again.

There was a noticeable difference in my brother when he returned. He was much more at peace with himself after his trip abroad. As soon as Bill returned, he brought over all of his pictures from the trip as well as brochures from many of the places he visited. He was so excited and invigorated from his trip; he decided the following year to fly to Grenada for a Windjammer cruise. He was ecstatic over this vacation. The food was delicious and the tropical drinks flowed throughout the day. Bill loved the sea after living in Cape Cod for many years where he owned a charter fishing boat. The Windjammer cruise was a chance for him to relive some of his memories on the ocean. The cruise was very informal. The guests would walk barefoot around the ship and also have small chores aboard the vessel such as assisting the crew with the rigging. Bill enjoyed it so much that he returned the following year for the same cruise. The people on board really catered to my brother because they never had someone 83 years old take part in one of their sailings. He would have sailed again on the cruise in 2004 but his legs started to fail him and he was afraid he would not have been able to keep his balance on the ship.

Instead of the Windjammer cruise, my brother decided to fulfill another one of his lifelong dreams. He had always wanted to visit Bavaria in Germany to attend an Octoberfest. So he hopped on a plane once again and spent 18 days in Europe. The trip was arranged through Trafalga Bus Tours and the people in the company took great care of him along the way. They always arranged for transportation for Bill when the distances were too much for him to walk. The trip took him to parts of Germany, France, Italy, and Switzerland. My brother always loved to have a beer or two, so his trip to Germany was a visit to the motherland. I was so happy for him to get this chance of a lifetime to visit Europe because I could see that his health was starting to decline.

Back home my brother's favorite hang out was the Coalminer's in Forest City. He used to arrive every afternoon at 3:30 to watch Who Wants to Be a Millionaire and have a couple of beers with his friends he met in town. At the end of March of 2006, Bill collapsed at the Coalminers, but refused to go to the hospital. He spent 10 days at my house trying to recuperate. He enjoyed me taking care of him every day and most of all he enjoyed sitting with my dog Rosie by his side on the couch. He finally went to a doctor who told him his lungs were filling up with fluid and if the medication did not take affect, he would only last a couple of days. Bill's health did improve for a short time and he gradually recovered from this episode and was able to go back to his home. The residents at the Penn Apartments commented that Bill had a little bit of a spring in his step and he greeted people with a cheery hello. However, I was concerned that he was getting one last "good spurt" of life and he would start to go down hill again. My fears were realized on May 24th, 2006, when I received a call from his apartment complex. They were concerned he had not gone out for his morning coffee. When they opened the door, Bill was found unconscious on the floor. An ambulance was called and he was rushed to the hospital and placed on life support. My daughter drove me to the hospital and according to Bill's wishes I made sure I had a copy of his living will. A CT scan revealed Bill had suffered a massive brain hemorrhage and had no chance of regaining consciousness. Per the Do Not Resuscitate order in his will, I requested that the life support be removed immediately. While I sat with Bill at the hospital, I kept rubbing his head and I told him, "Let go Bill, Hansy is waiting for you and all of your war buddies are waiting to see you."

The next day, on May 25th, my brother passed away at 6:00 pm. Not only was he my brother, he was my closest friend apart from my husband. I miss him terribly but at least I know he passed away peacefully and did not suffer. Even my dog Rosie misses him. She still waits on the porch looking out the window waiting for his car to pull up for his daily visit. My life has changed considerably, first losing my husband and then losing my brother.

But I am grateful for the seven wonderful years and the countless memories my brother and I shared in Forest City.

Bill did not want any type of funeral or memorial service. He did not even want his name listed on the obituary page of the local paper. His only request was to have his ashes spread out to sea on Cape Cod. I wanted to respect his wishes but I felt myself as well as his friends in Forest City needed some type of closure. I thought of a fitting tribute I know Bill would have approved. I posted a note at the Coalminer's Bar and let everyone know I was planning on having a toast to Bill on Friday evening, which was one week after he died. All of his friends were together from 7:00 to 9:00 and we had a wonderful time talking about Bill throughout the evening. I was touched to hear from many of his friends about how much he talked about me at the bar. They said his eyes would light up whenever he talked about me. It was such a good feeling for me to know how much we both thought of each other.

My brother did not have any easy life. He witnessed some terrible tragedies as well as the brutal experience of war. But in the end, he overcame all of these obstacles and I like to think he enjoyed and got more out of the last 7 years of his life than he did the first 75. In the end, neither one of us could have asked for anything more.

Printed in the United States
79663LV00005B/1-69